Angela
An Earth Angel's Journey

About the Author

Angela Young is a working Medium and Spiritual Healer. Overcoming her physical disabilities, she travels widely and uses her gifts to demonstrate that the soul within us all transcends the death of the physical body. She lives with her husband in the county of Kent, the renowned Garden of England. Angela Young is a pseudonym.

Angela
An Earth Angel's Journey

Angela Young

Angela
An Earth Angel's Journey

Olympia Publishers
London

www.olympiapublishers.com
OLYMPIA PAPERBACK EDITION

ISBN: 978-1-84897-759-4

First Published in 2016

Olympia Publishers
60 Cannon Street
London
EC4N 6NP

Printed in Great Britain

Dedication

I dedicate this book to my husband and to my friends Maria and Lorraine in gratitude for their support and for their encouragement.

CHAPTER 1

My story begins way before I was born. I want to tell you a little bit about the struggles our family went through and to give you an idea of why my mother and I reacted and behaved in the way we did.

My family came from an agricultural background, farm labourers, moving around to where ever they could find work. My mother Margaret Ingram was born in September 1934 to Elizabeth and Harold Ingram and was one of thirteen children, living in a two bedroomed council house. They had their fair share of tragedy, two of the children died within a few days of each other. Harold worked in the local paper mill and really did not look after his family; he tended to be found in the local pub drinking away his wages instead of providing for the family. Due to this, the council stepped in and warned him that if he didn't provide mattresses for the children they would be placed into care. Needless to say they were. Mum told me that at the age of six, a car turned up and took all of the children away with the exception of the eldest and the youngest and they were never to be reunited again as a whole family.

Mum was placed with a family living in Rochester in Kent, and they treated her terribly, beating her and making her do the housework before she went to school. One day, Mum came home from school and tried to let herself into the house only to find the doors were locked. She knocked and a woman answered and asked her what she wanted. Naturally Mum said she would like to come in but the woman turned round and said that she didn't live there anymore and promptly shut the door in her face.

You can only imagine how Mum would have reacted, she must have felt rather lost. She managed to get hold of the social worker dealing with her care and she was placed in a children's nursery where she was set to work looking after the other children. Then

Mum's life was turned upside down, she contracted TB (Tuberculosis) at the age of fifteen.

Whilst Mum was going through all of this, she had a wonderful relationship with her elder sister, Sandra. Sandra looked out for Mum in every which way even though they were not allowed to contact each other; Aunt Sandra defied the social workers and continued to look out for her sister.

Mum contracted TB twice, the first time was when she was aged fifteen and looking after children in a nursery and again when she was twenty. It was her second bout of T.B that led to an amazing experience.

This bout of T.B was accompanied by the dreaded addition of Meningitis; she 'died' and this was the story she told me:

> *I was laying on the bed and all of a sudden I felt myself lifting out of my body and floating towards the ceiling and I was looking down at my body. I felt very calm and peaceful. I turned and began walking up a dark tunnel towards the light at the end. The music and the love I felt was beautiful. When I got to the light, everywhere was bright and I was walking on the most beautiful green grass. In front of me was a white picket fence and a gate, I walked towards this and was just about to open the gate and a man appeared. He said that it was not time for me to die and that I was to go back. The next thing I remembered was being back in my body.*

Mum was in hospital for a long time recovering; she was placed in Preston Hall, Maidstone. When she was well enough to leave she had nowhere to go. The hospital offered her a place there to work and she was taken under a lady's wing. It was this lady that got Mum a place at St Thomas's hospital in London to train as a domestic servant. Aunty Sandra was still looking out for her and still defied the authorities by continuing to see Mum. Aunt Sandra managed to get mum to visit her parents. This had to be done secretly, and proved to be the last time Mum saw her parents. They both died within a couple of months of each other and were only in their mid-forties.

Mum's life seemed to be filled with a lot of heartache, of not being wanted, not being loved and being pushed from pillar to post. She was working at All Saints Hospital in Chatham when she walked into one of the doctor's rooms and found that he had committed suicide by slashing his wrist.

Time went on for Mum and one day she met my father. He was a cook at HMS Pembroke in Chatham Dockyard, the former naval base on the river Medway. He spun her a yarn, saying he was single and that he wanted to marry her. They got engaged and prepared for their wedding. Then her life was completely turned upside down. She told him one day that she was pregnant with his baby and he then went AWOL. The Military Police traced him to Scotland and they dragged him back to face the music. She then found out that he was already married with children but admitted that the baby was his. Due to this he was ordered to pay maintenance. I managed to obtain my records and it did show that he made some payments but these soon stopped. He clearly had no interest in me. I later found out from Mum that he only saw me once.

I was born in July 1956 after a very difficult and long labour. I also found out that Mum was living in Rochester then and I know that life was very difficult for her as an unmarried mother. She did tell me that she never ever wanted to give me up.

Mum later moved back in with Aunt Sandra and her husband, Harry. She was persuaded to go out as she was suffering from post natal depression. It was on one of these nights out that she met Eric Chapman. He courted her and finally she relented. She warned him that she already had a baby and he said that this would not change anything and that he still wanted to take her out.

They had been dating for a little while when Eric said that he wanted to get to know Mum and me better, so they decided to go on a day trip to Margate on the Thanet coast. Somehow they managed to miss the last train back to Chatham and Mum became fearful of going back home. They had no choice but to book into a boarding house for the night and it was then that they decided to go up to Derby. Aunt Sandra was absolutely frantic with worry as I'd not come home and they didn't have any clothes etc. for me.

It was whilst in Derby that Mum found out Eric's real age, he was only seventeen, he'd lied saying he was the same age as her; she was twenty two.

Eventually they returned and Eric went back home to his parents while Mum went to Aunt Sandra's. Eric still wanted to be with Mum and he then asked her to marry him to which she said yes. Due to his age, Eric's mother had suggested that they elope to Scotland; his father was not to know what was going on. Eric and Mum duly left for Scotland. In those days the ruling was that you had to live there for a short while before you could get married. It was whilst they were living in Scotland that Eric started seeing other women and the arguments started. Mum had soon had enough and packed her bags, going to the Salvation Army who helped her get back to Chatham. She wouldn't go back to her sister's house as she had discovered she was pregnant again and was frightened so she decided to stay in the Salvation Army Home.

When she found out she was pregnant she was terrified of telling her sister and didn't know what to do. By this time, Eric was once again on the scene. She told him she was expecting and he asked her to marry again. She reluctantly agreed. This time things were done differently. They sought his parents' permission and were married in February of 1958.

The arrangements they sorted out were as follows; Eric's parents' double fronted property in Gravesend, north Kent, had rooms in the attic. Mum and Eric were to live there and I was to live downstairs; Mum was not to have anything to do with me. I was kept strapped in a pram all day and my grandparents did not make any attempts to talk to or play with me. I was just ignored. The only interaction I had was my feed time and whenever I needed changing and that was whenever Eric's mother felt like doing it. I was therefore suffering from severe nappy rash because of this lack of care. The Social Services were very much involved and were keeping an eye on me.

My records noted that I was a pathetic and unloved child. Eric was also free with his fists and knocked my mother around too, with the approval of his mother. She wanted me and Mum got rid of and even said as much to the Social Worker.

Due to all the tension within the house, the Social Worker suggested that it would be best if I was adopted as this might help Mum and Eric's relationship. By this time my brother, David, had been born and he was a sickly child which added more pressure on a volatile relationship. Eric was still going out with other women and spending money on them. He was also still continuing to hit my mum. Life got very unbearable for her. Fortunately however there was a home not far away from where Mum was living, run by the Church of England's Children's Society. It was they who suggested that I should be adopted. After much heart searching mum agreed to let me go.

I was taken to Manchester. Mum was so upset after letting me go that she cried and begged for me to be brought back home. After about six months Eric relented and I came back home. Subsequently I paid the price for this.

Mum became pregnant with my sister, Anne, who was born in July 1959. Life was still unstable. Eric was still knocking mum around and mum kept going to the Church of England's Children's Society at Kendall House. They persuaded her to go back to her husband; it was a vicious circle. Eventually Mum and Eric left Gravesend and moved into a caravan in the remote Kent village of Hoo. This was a newly opened site housing caravans for people to live in. Unfortunately my life was about to take a turn for the worse.

Just a week after Anne was born, she was fostered out. The reason for this was that there was no room for her where Mum was living with Eric and that Eric didn't want Anne living with them, in fact he didn't want any children in the house. You can imagine how she was feeling; distraught at being separated from her baby. Anne was fostered out for a long time before she was able to go back to Mum. Eventually, after a struggle on Mum's part, she was allowed to go back home although the foster parents wanted to adopt her and

Mum put up a big fight. Sadly, shortly after this, Mum became ill with pneumonia and Anne was fostered out yet again. I believe Anne was eighteen months old before she was finally reunited with mum.

Going back to the caravan in Hoo, I don't remember too much of my time there; it's rather sketchy. Some of the information I have is from notes and piecing bits together.

We lived in a very small caravan painted red and cream on the outside. On one particular night, I could hear a lot of shouting going on in the next room. I was in the top bunk in the bedroom. I didn't sleep at all that night. I do know that something terrible had happened to me which I blocked out. I'd been beaten black and blue. I had cuts and bruises on my face and body and I was terrified. This was in April 1959 when I was nearly three years old. Someone in the next caravan had reported the incident to the NSPCC and I was immediately taken away and placed in protective care to get me away from danger. I wouldn't go near the doctor when he examined me, I screamed and ran away from him. Eric was arrested and charged with assault and he appeared before Northfleet magistrates' court in May. He was given a six month prison sentence but he immediately appealed on the grounds that he didn't deserve the sentence. He did go to prison, nevertheless.

Mum moved in with her brother and his German wife in Weedswood, Chatham and life there wasn't easy for any of us either. Mum became seriously ill again because she was malnourished and freezing cold; once again she ended up in hospital with pneumonia. This was the time when Anne was taken back into care. The next part I can only gather. Eric must have been released from prison and somehow he and Mum had decided to make a go of it again, I ask you!

This time, we moved into a much bigger caravan, painted green and white. I guess Eric realised that he had to behave himself by not being violent to us kids. He decided to get at me in another way. This time I was to be sexually abused.

I can remember having to go to bed with him and he made me do certain things to him. I never knew that what I was doing was wrong but he used to say, 'if you tell anyone what you have just done, you will be in for it'. You just didn't say anything for fear of being beaten again like I'd been before. This went on for years, up until the time when Mum left him and even then he still came to our house and followed the same routine. The abuse always happened when Mum wasn't around. I know this may sound silly, even today I will not wash myself with a flannel; this is due to Eric having a flannel by the side of the bed which he used it after he'd finished doing what he was doing. This used to give me flashbacks when I was a lot older.

There were so many things he used to do, not only to me but to my brother. I was made to watch whilst Eric dressed up my brother in girls' clothes and put ribbons in his hair. I will never forget my brother crying when Eric wouldn't stop what he was doing. He was cruel and nasty and laughed as he inflicted pain on us; gaining so much pleasure in doing so.

When I was about five years old, Mum started to notice that I wasn't responding to her when she spoke to me with my back to her. She decided to do a test and sure enough I didn't seem to be hearing very well. She took me to the doctors and then to All Saints Hospital in Chatham and later to the hearing department in Maidstone, where they discovered I was deaf. Years later, I found out my deafness was due to the beating I'd had from Eric. I was fitted with a hearing aid which was strapped to my body with a long wire connected to an earpiece. I needed to have speech therapy and they placed me in schools with special units that helped and taught you to speak.

Life continued on for a while. I do remember some good times, mostly with Mum. She had a wonderful wicked sense of humour and could be quite mischievous too. We'd lay in a poor farmer's corn field, flattening his crop, playing a game of hide and seek. She also played 'knock down ginger'; for which we kids got the blame, she would be acting all innocent and telling us off when the homeowner came out and gave us what for.

Living on the Hoo caravan site wasn't all a bundle of fun. There were some nasty people living there and their kids. My sister Anne was only about three when they put her on a plank of wood and set her afloat on the river Medway. She could have so easily drowned. Someone spotted her and Eric had to find a rowing boat quickly so he could rescue her.

I was playing in the nearby woods near a pond when all of a sudden I had a brick thrown at me which hit my head. My injuries could have been much worse than a cut to the head.

I went to the local infant's school in the village. This school had only a couple of classes and there was a round fire in the middle of the room to keep it warm. I didn't interact with the other children much because I couldn't hear them very well in any case if they found out you came from the caravan site you were considered an outsider. When I got to junior school, I was picked up every day and taken to Barnsole Road School in Gillingham. The one memorable thing about that school was being picked to play Noddy in a school play and wearing the blue hat. It was a long way travelling from Hoo to Gillingham and I didn't get back home till late afternoon.

It used to take an hour to get to Chatham by bus and we had to make the journey to visit All Saints Hospital there for my hearing assessments. The village of Hoo was quite small, it had a school, church, pub, a few shops and a doctors' surgery. It was a nice place to live in, but now Hoo has expanded quite a bit and there is a housing estate and more shops. To get to my school from the caravan site, we used to have to walk a long way by going across a field and through a church yard, the school was next to the church. It's now the local library.

One of my memories of the shops was going to a hairdressers. I used to have very long wavy hair almost down to my waist and it was Eric who told Mum to get it all cut off. I loved my hair and I was heartbroken when I sat in the hairdressers and watched all of my curls falling to the floor. I never grew my hair long again.

This period didn't last long because things were about to change again.

The next chapter in my life began when we moved in with Eric's parents in Beltinge, Herne Bay on the north Kent coast. Why we moved there I don't know. I think I can remember Mum saying that it was to enable them to save their money and buy their own house. We moved in and it was a very big house that was at the end of the road which was at the cliff edge. This house used to have two garages and two tennis courts, one of each ended up in the sea; that's how close we were to the edge. It had a massive big garden and that was where we spent most of our time when the weather was good.

We children had to sleep, eat and play in one room, while Eric and Mum had another. Opposite our room was a bathroom which had two little dogs living in it. They never came out of it much, in fact they died in there and I remember Eric's mother burning them on the bonfire.

We three children had to stay in the same room every day and we just had a small cardboard box with some toys in it. I know his sounds stupid, but all I can remember about that box is the smell of coffee which somehow had got into it.

Eric was still coming into the room in the middle of the night and taking me into his bed. I don't know where Mum was when this was going on. I do know that she used to work in a sweet factory, but I'm not sure if she was working nights. She was blissfully ignorant of what was going on. It was many years later that I summoned up the courage to tell her and her reaction was to become very angry – at not knowing what had been going on and angry with Eric for what he had done to me. I never did reveal to her the full extent of what he did.

Life was cruel living with Eric's parents at Beltinge. They made Mum's and our lives hell. They used to trip Mum over when she was carrying our food on a tray to bring it to us. We then had to eat it after it had ended up on the floor. Our washing was pulled off the line and trampled into the mud. We were given chicken soup for our lunch one day and all three of us were violently sick for a few days and we learnt that they had put something nasty in it. We were taunted and abused in so many ways; this is just a tip of the iceberg of what they did to us.

Living in this house were Eric's two sisters and a brother along with his mother and father. Alan was the worse one for cruelty along with Eric. But then there could be a nicer side to him; he taught me how to fire a rifle and he showed me his drawings which were beautiful. He certainly was a gifted man. I don't know what he used to do for a living. One of Eric's sisters was having an affair with a married man and she fell pregnant with his child. They used to sit out in the car talking a lot of the time. The other sister was kinder, she just got on with her own life and didn't bother with anyone.

Eric's mother was also a cruel woman. I didn't like her at all, there was just something about her that exuded hatred. She did show a little tender side to her, she showed me her collection of dolls that she kept in her bedroom and she had a button tin whereby she showed me all these special buttons. Eric's father was a strange man, he didn't interact with anyone. In fact I don't remember him speaking to me. He may have done, but it was rare. I do recall him having had an accident whilst gardening; he put a garden fork right through his foot, ouch!

They also had an Alsatian dog called Rover; one minute he was there the next he was gone. I asked what had happened to him and Eric said that he'd got run over by a train. How that had happened I don't know because we were a long way from the railway.

The house at Beltinge was very dark, with old antiques and furniture; I believe Eric's parents used to buy and sell furniture although I really didn't know what they did to earn their money. One particular memory that stands out is one Christmas time, when we were allowed into the 'best room'. This was full of old furniture, animal rugs on the floor and dead animals' heads hanging on the wall. I used to be so scared of walking through the door with those eyes watching me. There was a television in the corner of the room and we were allowed to watch the programmes. This was a treat for us as we were not normally allowed to watch television. That was the one and only time that I went into that room.

Life at Beltinge wasn't all doom and gloom. We children did manage to have some good times. Right near us in the next road was a larger stream than the one we had in front of the house where we were living, which had model houses in the water. Beside the stream was a shop that used to sell ice cream. A lot of people didn't know that there was a lovely sandy beach there which was accessible by going down wooden steps. We managed to get there once and had a lovely time. We also went to a school in Reculver and I can honestly say that it was one of the best schools I've ever been to. This school was next to a very old church and the teachers and headmaster were really kind people. We had to travel by bus to get to this school and there were times that we decided to save some money by walking home across the fields. There was one occasion that we were walking across a farmer's field and hadn't noticed there was a bull. By the time we did we had to leg it; we just got over the hedge before it got us. It was scary at the time but every time I think about it, I just have to titter to myself. We did get found out as the farmer came round and had a word with Eric, as a result we got punished by being sent to bed with no tea.

Overall, living in Beltinge was not a happy time for us all, but one afternoon Mum came home from work early. There wasn't anyone else in the house, only us children. She told us to hurry and get as much stuff together as we could, then we went outside and there was Mum's brother with his big cement lorry. The cab was just big enough to hold us all with our belongings. It was a squeeze but we didn't care as we were escaping to start our new life.

CHAPTER 2

We arrived tired in Rainham, Kent at my maternal uncle's flat. He lived above a car show room and obviously we couldn't stay there. We then went to my Aunt Sandra's house in Chatham. Again she had made room for us with open arms. I really enjoyed being there. I felt safe. I couldn't understand why, but I just knew I was safe. We all had to double up by sharing beds, my aunt and uncle really didn't have room for us all but they couldn't see us out in the streets.

I had some really happy times there. I played with toys. My favourite was Lego, the bricks were grey, white and red – not like the Lego of today where you can do so much with them. Watching TV, my favourite was Come Dancing, seeing all those beautiful dresses. Colour television wasn't out then. I also loved going out to play without worrying what was happening indoors. One November we went to see the torchlight procession in Chatham town, buying a bag of chips and sharing. We had a lot of laughter. My Uncle Harry was a very special man too. He came from Yugoslavia and he used to do a lot of the cooking and introduced us to some wonderful flavours such as stuffed cabbage, stuffed peppers, and he did this wonderful cheese pastry that was of thin layers. Mum asked him one day what it was called and he said 'Uncle Peter's leg' as he used to love pulling her leg. That name stuck whenever we were going to have this treat. Poor Mum didn't have a choice with regards to food as she had to feed us on whatever she could get her hands on and I know there were many times she went without so that we had something to eat.

Where my aunt and uncle lived was in a valley. There were hills on both sides of the road. Opposite their house was the butchers, down the road slightly more on the same side as us was the fish and chip shop. Up the road on three corners were shops such as the newsagents and post office. On the opposite corner was a small shop that sold different things – all old fashioned, cheese and butter were wrapped, sugar put into a bag. On the third corner was another bigger grocery store. All of that has gone now, the big shops have destroyed the sense of community. If they call that progress, then it hasn't worked. It has alienated everyone.

At the top of Gladstone hill was a big house. It had been empty for years and five of us used to go there and play hide and seek. One day I was hiding behind a bush and hadn't noticed a metal bar with a hook on it. I ran out and caught my knee on the hook and tore a big hole in my knee. Blood was going everywhere. My cousin, Ann, went running home to fetch my Uncle Harry and he came to fetch me, looked at my injuries and carried me all the way to St. Bartholomew Hospital on the New Road in Chatham. He didn't stop once, he wanted to get me there as soon as possible. I had my knee sewn up followed by a tetanus injection.

Our happiness wasn't to last long; it couldn't with all of us living under one roof. The council wouldn't rehouse us and the situation was made difficult because my aunt and uncle owned their own house. The only way around this situation was for them to evict us. I know this broke my aunt's heart but she didn't have a choice and it was the only way we could get a home.

We were sent to live in a hostel in West Malling. This was a place where no men were allowed to stay. It was a bit like living in an army barracks, but there were separate living quarters. Ours was right at the end of the building and to us kids it was an adventure. You went through one door into a small passageway, off of this were two bedrooms with hospital beds in them. You then went into the main room which housed the kitchen with a range and off that room was another bedroom which was Mum's. I know that when we got there Mum burst out crying; she was really at a low ebb.

We soon settled in and made the most of it. Mum managed to cook some fantastic stews on that range and other meals too. There were times when she just didn't have any money to feed us; she might just have some jam, suet and flour. With this she made us dumplings and boiled them in water and we ate them with jam in the middle. I tell you, they were absolutely delicious.

There were two other families living in our hut. We all had to share the bathrooms and toilet and each family were responsible for cleaning them in turn. We soon made friends on the site. It was massive, as there were rows and rows of these huts filled with families waiting for somewhere to live. At the back behind the hostel was an airfield where the planes used to take off and land in the Second World War and behind the wall were the abandoned huts and buildings. We were told not to go anywhere near them, but you can guess that we ignored these warnings. We had such fun climbing in and out of these buildings; it's a wonder that we never had an accident, and there was one waiting to happen.

I went to a school which had a hearing unit at Molehill Copse in Maidstone and I remembered one day there was a lot of excitement in the air. We had a camera crew come into the school film us in the classrooms and the playground. I was seen hanging upside down on the climbing bars in the playground. Later that week the film was shown on the TV; fame at last!

We really loved living where we were, it was in the country. It was quite a walk into West Malling village but we didn't mind, it was all good fun. I don't think we were made welcome by the village people, as you were 'scum' if you came from the hostel. West Malling at that time was rather a posh area where well to do people lived and they just didn't want the likes of us there lowering the tone. They just considered us as thieves and immoral people. They didn't look at the fact that many people were not as lucky as them and that life had dealt them hard blows.

There was one tragic incident which occurred. My sister Anne's best friend went to the main road to wait for her mum to come home by bus, she was so excited that she ran out into the road and was instantly killed. This caused a riot within the camp.

Following the accident, the women wanted to stage a demonstration and throw stones at passing cars. Mum refused to take part and because of this they made her life hell. They did some awful things to her and us but she wouldn't give in. This tragedy caused such a commotion and stirring of anger that the newspapers got hold of the story and a film crew came to the camp; on the day when the film crew arrived, I was sitting up in the oak tree watching all of this taking place below. Thankfully the hoo-hah died down and it wasn't long before we were packing our belongings yet again. We were moving into our first home.

We moved into a three bedroomed house on the White Road Estate in Chatham. We had no furniture or bedding, just an empty house, but it was our home. I will always remember that house. On the day we got there, an old rickety lorry turned up with some furniture on it for us. There was a settee, beds and a table and Mum was given a grant to buy our bedding and pillows. It was such a happy occasion, we were all laughing and skipping around as we went into town to buy all we needed.

What I haven't told you is what happened when we got into the house. Mum walked through the living room into the kitchen. To the left of the kitchen was an old cooker and sitting on a chair by the cooker was an old man wearing trousers, vest and braces holding up his trousers. As you can imagine, this caused Mum such a fright that she shouted at him to go away. The man was a ghost. I don't know if Mum had any more experiences of 'spiritual happenings' at White Road Estate; she never said.

My sister and I used to share a double bed in the front bedroom, my brother had the opposite room and mum slept in the middle room. I was so happy living there, being a normal kid and not having to walk on eggshells. It was great that 'he' wasn't around. Once again Eric had made promises to Mum and once again he broke them. He did turn up a couple of times and, you guessed it, he took me to bed. He did this whilst Mum was working as a cleaner in an office. That was the very last time he did anything to me because he went away and I later found out he'd fathered a child with another woman and I believe he moved up towards the North.

We all soon got into a routine living in our home. I do know that Mum filed for a divorce and she had to do a lot to protect herself from Eric. She was eventually granted her divorce; in the 60s this was a difficult process. The first thing Mum did when she came out of the courts was to take her wedding ring off and throw it as far as she could. She was now a free woman.

I went to the local Glencoe Road School which was just across the road from where I was living. It was just like any other establishment, only at this school I had special tutoring from a Mr White who gave me speech therapy. I really got on well with him and he used to visit our house and in doing so he got to know Mum. He took us out to the country once and we all really liked him and my daft bat of a mother refused his proposal of marriage; her reason being she felt he was above her. I could have slapped her. If only she'd married Mr White, it might have saved the heartache that was yet to come.

There was one funny incident. In those days, the council used to decorate the rooms. We were having a bedroom done and the man had finished the work for the day. I'd been upstairs talking to him and came down the stairs in front of him. He was carrying the glue bucket and brush and he didn't see that there was a kitten on the stairs. One minute it was daylight and the next – dark! I just screamed and Mum came running out to the hall saw me with a bucket over my head and glue running down all over me. She, being a very concerned and caring mother, burst out laughing. The poor man was mortified! The kitten made itself scarce! It took a long while to get the glue out of my hair. All the time Mum still kept laughing.

I thought my abuse had stopped. I think because of the situation of us having to be rehoused and what had happened to Mum, we had a Social Worker come and visit us and I also think he was something to do with therapy of some sort. He took us upstairs without Mum and used to talk to Anne; not sure about my brother. But when it came to me, it was different.

One day, he told me to kneel by the side of the bed and read the book out loud to him. I then felt him pull down my knickers and felt 'this thing' being rubbed against me; being naïve I had no idea of what he was doing. Later, I discovered he was rubbing his penis against me. When he finished he told me that I was a 'good girl' and gave me sixpence and was told I wasn't to mention anything to anyone. We didn't see him again, I wonder why?

There is just something about some men and I seem to have attracted them. There was another man who had a shed and he used to take me there to show me his dirty books. Why oh why do some men have to do this thing to children? It just makes me so mad; I just didn't realise what they were doing was wrong and just thought it was normal.

All this had a devastating effect on me years later when Esther Ranzten did a TV programme on child abuse. Suddenly it hit me that what they were doing was so wrong. I went to pieces. It had such an effect on me that it affected my relationship with my husband, I became angry and couldn't believe that grown men were allowed to do this. I was just an innocent child who didn't know what they were doing was so wrong.

I grew up believing that I didn't have a voice and just had to accept what was happening to me and not say 'no' and fight back. Even today I find it difficult to voice my thoughts, but slowly I'm getting there. We children were expected to never answer back nor ask questions. In my case, if I should ever do so, the fear was that I was going to get a beating. So I never opened my mouth but this affected my emotions as I didn't understand why I reacted or behaved the way I did as I grew older.

I used to love going to Saturday morning pictures and was always on the lookout for a boyfriend; my hormones were beginning to kick in as I was eleven years old. I went to the pictures on this particular morning and saw a boy I fancied little realising that I would meet him again years later and marry him.

There was one special act of kindness. Where Mum used to work as a cleaner at the Reliance Building Society in Chatham, she befriended a lady who worked there as a cashier. The lady was married but didn't have any children at the time and she offered to take us three children for a day trip to Hastings. Mum's friend, Billie, made clothes and she made me a dress which was yellow and cream. It had big flowers on it and the sleeves were 'bell sleeves' and the hem of the dress was short, this was the 60s. I just couldn't sleep the night before we were due to go out as I was so looking forward to wearing the dress, it was a special dress to me

Mum started to go out on dates. She had penfriends and often she would meet up with them. There was one man she met who lived in Ramsgate and they seemed to get on really well until she fell pregnant and once again, he deserted her. She was left to go through it all alone and gave birth to my brother Darren in 1968.

In 1967 I left Glencoe Road School and went to Highfields Secondary School, which also had a Hearing Unit. I made some great friends and not so great friends. Some of the children were quick to think I was stupid and backward just because I was deaf and their cruelty has affected me ever since. It was my ears that I had a problem with, not my brain! Even in the Unit I couldn't escape from sexual abuse as there was a male teacher who gave me special tutoring and at the same time made sexual advances. I hated him for it.

I got on with my education. I loved English and Drama but hated maths as we had the most boring maths teacher who used to send us to sleep by going off the subject and talking gibberish. I even put in a complaint about him and asked to be moved to another class, but to no avail.

In 1971 I could have left school but I chose to stay on for the fifth year. If you did so you were considered as an adult and could choose what to wear. In that year it was the Mods and Rockers and we chose the style of the Mods. Was it worth staying on an extra year? Yes, it was for me. I got a certificate at the end of it and it showed I worked hard to get it and I suppose I wanted to prove to myself I wasn't the stupid idiot that people said I was.

Going back a little bit here, behind the house in Pretoria Road was an allotment where my Uncle Harry had a large plot. He grew his own vegetables which was handy for Mum as he used to supply her with some. I really loved Uncle Harry; there was something very gentle and kind about him. He didn't say a lot, he didn't need to, and you just knew you were loved. If only he had been my real father.

I don't know why, but Mum decided to move again. This time we moved to Wayfield Estate. My body was going through turmoil as I was thirteen and puberty was kicking in big-time. I tried to get involved in things at the school like helping with the fete, school sports etcetera. I was looking to be accepted and to find my niche. It was the December of 1969 when I lost someone I loved.

Mum had gone out into the garden to get some washing in off the line. She looked up and noticed a very bright star that was moving across the sky and then disappeared. She came in and told me about it and we didn't think any more of it. About an hour later there was a knock on the door and standing there was my cousin. She was crying and when Mum finally calmed her down we were told that my beloved Uncle Harry had died earlier that day of a massive heart attack. I was very upset, so I plucked up the courage to speak to my English teacher and he lashed out at me saying I had no right to be upset as Uncle Harry wasn't my father and that I was being selfish for not thinking of my cousins who'd lost their dad. That was a lot of comfort for me – I don't think.

I didn't get a chance to go and pay my respects as it was not the done thing in those days to have children at funerals and I don't know where Uncle Harry is buried to this day.

It was a few days later that we were moving again. This time we moved to Weedswood Estate, in the very same road I lived in when I was coming up to three after I'd been beaten. This time we were further up the road. Weedswood Estate was okay then but there were some rough families living there and one family in particular were notorious.

We tried to get on with life but you did have to keep your wits about you. We had our window smashed when a brick was thrown through it. Luckily no one was near the window. Mum did call the police and it seemed to have sent out the message that you don't mess around with my mum, because it quietened down after that. My brother used to help a guy on his milk round and go out fishing with him. It's like this man took him under his wing.

Being such a shy person, whenever I fancied a boy, I used to get my sister to give him a note saying I fancied him. I'm sure that many of you who are reading this story did the same thing. Anyway, I used to notice this boy who used to collect for Cancer and Polio Research where you paid so much a week to take part in a draw. On this particular day he got the 'note'. It was May 1970. He agreed to see me and we went for a walk and got on really well. He wanted to take me out on a date to a cinema. The amazing thing is that he was the very boy I fancied years previously in the cinema. His name was Martin.

We did have a bit of a disastrous start to our relationship. We agreed to meet at a particular bus stop and I was so, so excited to be going out and that Mum had agreed that I could go. I got to the bus stop and waited, and waited and waited some more, but Martin didn't turn up. As you can imagine I was really upset. What we both didn't realise was that I hadn't heard him correctly. Martin didn't know for some time that I was deaf. He was waiting at another bus stop some distance away as he was afraid that his parents would disapprove of me because of the age gap. We did finally sort out the misunderstanding.

Talking about him not knowing I was deaf, every time we got a bit amorous with our kissing my hearing aid used to whistle. When I did finally tell him about my disability he floored me by saying that had he known I was deaf he wouldn't have gone out with me. However, by this time he'd fallen in love with me.

After a while, Martin thought it was about time he introduced me to his family, he was worried because he was three years older than me. Martin's family accepted me and I used to go up to their house at weekends. There was a bit of a social divide as I came from a council estate and he lived in a lovely bungalow. Martin's family had a car and telephone; we had nothing.

From the age of fourteen I managed to get a Saturday job and earned my own money from which I saved up and bought my own clothes. It was really difficult for Mum as she was a cleaner earning very little. What she had had to go on rent and food. There were the usual ups and downs; once I absolutely lost my temper, which is rare for me. I got so fed up with my brother and I fighting that I chased him around the house with a broom handle, he shut the door on me and the broom went through the back of it and then he ran into the toilet upstairs. I just lost it and slammed my hand through the window.

I had a tiny nick and to say my brother left me alone after that, it was a blessing. Mum never found out about the hole in the door until years later and then we just said we pushed the door open too hard. We all muddled together and just got on with it. There was a lot of unrest in the 70s with strikes, power cuts etc., but I really didn't notice much as I was just a kid.

Whilst we were living in Weedswood, Mum was writing to a man whom I later come to know as Henry. We met him and he seemed quite nice but there was something strange about him and I couldn't put my finger on it at the time. He asked Mum to marry him and they were married in September 1970 and we had a fantastic party afterwards. Let's just say there was a few sore heads the next morning and a broken window that Martin had fallen through.

And guess what? We were packing boxes again and we moved to Chatham where my school was behind us. Martin and I were seeing each other nearly every day then and we were beginning to get on each other's nerves so I said why don't we see each other on a Wednesday and at weekends. This worked out really well. It gave us more freedom to do other things. He used to ride a motor bike and we went to a few places on it once he passed his test.

When we had lived in Pagitt Street for a couple of months, I turned up at home after being out with Martin for the day to find Eric there. I was shocked to see him as I didn't want to have anything to do with him, I didn't stay for long, but I wondered why he was there. I think from what I was told, he wanted to see if he could get Mum back; no chance. We never saw him again. When I'd found out from my sister that he'd died in 2012/13 the relief I felt was enormous. I just cried with happiness. He had tried communicating with me through a Spiritualist Medium asking for my forgiveness as he was sorry. He said that he wanted to make amends and he wanted to put things right so that he could go into the light. I wouldn't grant him his wish and he said he realised it would take a lot for him to redeem himself. The Medium picked up on a very evil energy and it was making her uncomfortable; I just knew straight away who it was. He was stuck in-between worlds and I said I would never ever forgive him. He was only asking for his own selfish reasons not because he wanted to atone for what he had done. He has tried on a couple of occasions to get through to me, but for once I feel I have the power over him. I know that may sound strange because of what I know now, but when you have gone through so much torment during your life and the voice and power has been taken away, it's so nice to have that power over him. Maybe I'll forgive him in time, but then it will only be done when I've gone back home to the Spirit World.

CHAPTER 3

I left school on the last day of my exams in May 1972; free at last! I can't say school was all bad because it wasn't. I just made the most of it and did my best. I don't know if my mum was ever proud of me for doing well as any decisions I had to make concerning my future were mine.

I did have a teacher coming up to me saying 'well done'. Puzzled, I asked why as I was never in his class. He said that he'd just found out that I was deaf and he never knew. He told me what attracted me to him was my smile as I was always smiling and he said that I was to continue on with it. Funny how small things stick in your mind.

What can I say about my schooling? Well, I'd made friends for as long as they want to know you, the usual playground bullying, the 'favourite' girl, and the boys who were always trying to get into your knickers – why? I did have some taunts and abuse because I was deaf. People said I was stupid and that I would never amount to anything in my life; even the Social Workers said the same thing. Children can be so cruel and even today, at school nothing changes.

I enjoyed sport; the taking part not the watching so much. I did manage to get my place on sports day and did quite well. I loved swimming, rounders and netball. The teachers weren't bad either; they did their best in teaching us. There was one special boy and we did fall in love but his mother was the school governor. She found out about our relationship and I couldn't understand one day why he was so distant from me. We did contact each other many years later and he told me what had happened. She didn't approve of her son, who was the school captain and excelled in sports etc. being seen with 'that girl who's deaf and comes from a low background'. Needless to say that hurt.

Anyway, I'd left school and was waiting for September to come as I'd been given a place at Brixton College to a do secretarial course. It was the Social Workers who found me the place; why flipping Brixton I don't know. It was a hell of a journey every day and caused me tremendous stress. On one occasion I caused excitement to my fellow travellers by collapsing with a violent headache which was later diagnosed in hospital as a migraine brought on by the daily stress of travelling. I did get a job working in the Education Dept. in Maidstone whilst waiting to start college. I'd only completed one year as I just couldn't hack the train journey every day and on top of that I couldn't take my Pitman 2 exam as I was the sole candidate who could take it. I was more advanced than the others as I'd already had a head start with the typing from when I was in the fifth year at school. I didn't see any point in staying on.

My time at the college was fun apart from the travelling. I used to go out at lunch time to the pub; (not all the time I hasten to add). I made some great friends, went out ice skating and to different places. I did have quite a few boys chasing after me, some fell in love with me but it was difficult to explain away why there were roses being delivered to the house, I just said that they were for Mum and she went along with it, but I was dating Martin still. Mind you I did go out with a couple of them but they knew I had a boyfriend and nothing else was going to come of it. I was even made captain of badminton and I know I was good at it. At the college we played volley ball and I loved that too.

It's funny when you think about it, I was accepted at the college. No one made fun of me or treated me like an idiot; they really were a lovely bunch of people. I wonder where they are today.

After leaving college when I decided I'd had enough, I thought I'd better get on and find a job. I managed to find one working for Securicor in their Data Department. At first it was going to be based in Chatham but then they decided to move it to Maidstone. I couldn't drive and it made it rather difficult for me getting there but I managed to do it. I worked in that department for a while, and then I heard there was a position opening for a Business and Sales Administrator and Branch Secretary. I was responsible for the profits and loss of the branch, dealing with the Bank of England and so on.

It was interesting and challenging work. After I'd worked there for a while I applied for the position of Branch Secretary of the Alarms Division. Sounds posh but the working conditions were appalling. I worked in a porta cabin in the back yard – not nice.

Working at Securicor had other benefits. I went to Brands Hatch Racing Circuit to work as a security guard. I was placed on the Grosvenor Suite door with another guard. This suite was the celebrity suite where all the stars of the day used to watch the races. I met Alvin Stardust, Dave Lee Travis, Bay City Rollers, the late Errol Brown, Noel Edmunds, Pans People, The Rubettes, the late James Hunt and many others. I've still got their autographs. There was one Radio presenter called Alan Freeman who gave me a big kiss, yuk! It was wonderful working there.

I also did work at Gatwick Airport where, even then, we hand searched hand luggage for any likely weapons such as scissors or nail files. I found this work interesting as you met all kinds of people from around the world there was some laughter too. You just won't believe what people pack in their bags! I've also seen money, lots and lots of money, when I worked in the wage packet department making up wage packets for employees. All that has changed now I think. Not many people receive wages in cash; it's all done by bank transfer.

Even in my workplace I was being verbally taunted, which I didn't realise for quite a while afterwards. It was from one particular man who was in charge of the guard dogs. I guess for once I was lucky that I didn't hear him most of the time.

In 1974 Martin asked me to marry him and I said yes. He presented me with a beautiful engagement ring which was white gold with a sapphire in the middle and diamonds surrounding it. We were at a Tesco's work do in Wainscott on the outskirts of the Medway towns when he asked me to marry him. All of his work colleagues were over the moon for us and I can remember the band playing a song, which is my favourite, Spanish Eyes. I went home to Mum at the end of the evening and was tapping my finger on the back of the chair trying to get my mum's attention on the ring when she finally noticed; she was overjoyed for us.

Now we had to save up for the wedding as Mum really couldn't afford to pay for all of it. I earned extra money by doing overtime in different jobs within Securicor and Martin got extra overtime working at Tesco's. Martin's parents helped us with the cost of the wedding. I made the bridesmaid dresses and found ways of trying to do things cheaply. Martin and I went to the Rochester market, it was a big market back in the '70s and bought the materials for the dresses. We put it all back in the car and went off to go and buy other things. It was such a shock to us when we returned to find that our car had been stolen. We were very lucky as the car was later found intact but everything else was gone, we had to find more money and start again. You know, they say you can have very memorable years and 1974 was one of the best for me. The week before my wedding I went on a hen night to a restaurant above a pub in Railway Street in Chatham. We had a great night and needless to say I was a little drunk. I fell down the last few steps on the stairs at the bottom. I also flashed my knickers walking up Railway Street at a passing car, and I truly am sorry if you happen to have been that driver!

When I got home I had a wonderful surprise; my brother Jason was there waiting for me to come home. He'd joined the Queen's Regiment and was in their band and he had managed to get time off to be with me on my wedding day.

I woke up early and Mum had made me a very special breakfast and brought it up to me to eat in bed. It was a very special moment for us as she was losing her daughter and I was taking the next big step of my life by becoming a wife. Whilst I was at the hairdressers an old lady who was having her hair done at the same time as me had overheard that I was getting married that day. She came over to me and wished me luck and gave me a small present. It was a rain hat in a small purse, it was a beautiful gesture coming from a total stranger. 1976 was also the hottest year and we had a water shortage and everywhere was so dry and the grass was yellow.

After everyone had left for the church and before Mum left, I did turn to her and said 'am I doing the right thing?' But it turned out that I was. I guess I was having a wobbly moment and I daresay I won't be the last to have had one of those.

My stepfather, Henry, was to give me away and we left for the church. The wedding and reception were wonderful; it really couldn't have come together any better as we all had a wonderful time. We had our honeymoon on a caravan holiday park at Burnham-on-Sea in Somerset. We had a good start to our honeymoon, we had a row! I was reading the map and told Martin to turn right out of the hotel car park and he argued that we had to go left. He soon realised that he was wrong. Never argue with someone who has the map and yes I can read them.

We were also waiting for our house completion contract as we'd bought a house in Lordswood. It arrived on the morning of the wedding and Martin had brought it with him so that we could sign it and send it off. The house was only a year old, it had a drive up to the front with a car port attached to the front of the house, door entrance to the hall with stairs going up to the two bedrooms. There was the living room which led into the kitchen/diner. Out back was the garden with a flowering cherry tree and lots and lots of flint stones.

We moved into our first home; it was wonderful to me as it was something that was 'ours'. It was my very first proper home. All we had by way of furniture was mum's old settee with the spring gone in the middle, a television that you had to bang when the sound got too loud, a bed that somehow developed bed bugs, {nasty things), which meant we had to have the house fumigated. I had no washing machine and had to do it all by hand. When I was given a mangle I had to drag it in from outside every time I used it. As time went on we managed to upgrade to a twin tub and eventually an automatic. Freezers were just starting to come in and our first one was an old ice cream freezer which we kept outside under the carport with an iron bar and padlock across it to stop anyone stealing our food, but they were good memorable days.

We celebrated our first wedding anniversary by Martin throwing a surprise party and presenting me with twelve red roses, one for each month, and other presents. He took me to Maidstone so that the rest of the family could get the food and house ready; I just didn't have a clue but it was wonderful.

Then my happiness was to change again.

I was having driving lessons and really enjoying them because I'd always wanted to own my own car and drive wherever I wanted to go without having to worry about public transport. I was nearing my driving test when the driving instructor asked me to read a number plate in front and I had a bit of a struggle. He therefore suggested I go and get my eyes tested, which I did.

After I'd had my eyes examined I thought I would just have a pair of glasses. The optician turned to me and said that he would like a specialist to have a look at my eyes as he'd seen something he was not sure of. I was to wait for an appointment from Moorfield Eye Hospital in London.

I will always remember that day for the rest of my life. It was September 1977. I'd just had my twenty-first birthday and Mum and I went to London. I was wearing a white dress and looked the 'bee's knee's'. We were called into the consulting room and the room was filled with students and other doctors, I thought 'aye aye, what's happening here?' He explained why they were there as he was teaching them and then all the tests began. I was later sent downstairs to have a dye injected into my arm so they could photograph the back of the eyes and retina.

Eventually after being at the hospital for hours I was called back into the room and when I was given the diagnosis, it absolutely floored me. I was just numb, and wasn't able to take in what the specialist had just said.

He looked at me and said, 'I'm sorry but it's not good news. I'm afraid you have a rare disease called Retinitis Pigmentosa, the condition means that you are going blind and there is nothing we can do for you'. He said he didn't know how quickly I would lose my sight, but thought I would be blind within twenty-five years. This condition is hereditary and so far as I know I'm the only person in my family to have it, (I don't know anything about my father's side of the family). It could be passed onto my children and I was therefore advised to think seriously about having them.

RP is a condition where the retina crumbles and you have black floaters swimming across your vision. You can suffer by either losing your sight from the outside in or the opposite way. You can also wake up one day and be completely blind. There are about 200 types of the disease and within those 200 are another 200. Finding a cure is very difficult for this condition. I do have one saving grace and that is my deafness – Ushers Syndrome – it cannot be passed on. RP also means that I suffer with night blindness, which explains why I have difficulty in seeing in the dark. I also have difficulty in working out colours; my eyes see one colour and it's only when I ask someone about the colour that my brain 'see's that colour.

It was also on this occasion that Mum finally told me my father's real name; even then she lied. The bit she got right was his name, John Young, but she said he was a Canadian and an officer. I don't know who she was protecting, me or herself. I will tell you here, I was ten when she told me that Eric was not my real father. I went and told my best friend and she turned round and said that this made me a 'bastard'. I just shrugged my shoulders as I'd never heard of the word let alone knew what it meant.

I was numb when Mum and I travelled home from Moorfields. I kept looking out of the window of the train as there were several times when I nearly broke down and cried; let's just say my lips got sore with the biting to stop the tears flowing. I told Martin my news and it felt as if something was shut off between us. I didn't know what his thoughts were because I don't think we ever really spoke about it. I just got on with life.

Three and a half years after we were married, I became pregnant with my first child. I was so over the moon. It was a good pregnancy and I looked forward to the baby being born. In those days we were not offered scans to find out what the sex of the baby was. I think I got my first clue when I won a first prize on the raffle at a New

Year's function and it was a big pink teddy bear we called Boozy as it was hand-made. Its eyes were wonky, arms floppy and we just fell in love with it; Amy still has the bear today.

I went into labour on 20th January 1980 and my darling daughter was born on 21st January. We named her Amy Louise Porter. She was an absolute darling sweet baby. I remember that I was left alone with her in my room at the hospital and she was laying in my arms. She had beautiful features, all her fingers and toes and dark hair. I vowed that I would always be there for her and not let anyone harm her. How distraught I was so many years later when I felt that I had so let her down. I will say here, the food in the hospital was awful. It was three days after I'd given birth, my milk was coming through and I was in a lot of pain and my hormones were all over the place. I went upstairs to the dining room in the hospital to eat my dinner and when they placed it in front of me I just burst out crying. So would you if you were given spam and baked beans!

Now, I did say Amy was a sweet baby. Yes she was until six p.m. came, then all hell let loose! Martin used to come home at six, she then opened her mouth and cried solidly for four hours. We just could not get her to settle; we burped her, changed her, and bathed her all to no avail. We'd even drive around hoping to lull her to sleep. God, those first few months were a torment. Then she goes and sleeps all day. I'm sure there are some parents reading this who know exactly what I'm talking about.

We got into a routine as a family unit. I did have to stop certain members of the family trying to take over whenever I was doing anything; in the end I had to tell them to stop. They were thinking I was blind already and not allowing me to live a normal life. When Amy was about two we were on the move as we needed a bigger house because I wanted another child and we were living in a two bedroomed house.

We moved into our new house. It was really lovely and we settled in. We really enjoyed ourselves with our daughter. I had two part time jobs. One was cleaning and the other working in a clothes shop upstairs in the Pentagon shopping centre in Chatham. I started to get broody so I sort of begged Martin for us to have another baby and not long afterwards I became pregnant again. It was exactly three years and three weeks after Amy was born that Steven was born. He was a lovely baby too. He was a little bit like Amy when it came to bedtime but I soon got that sorted. I had learnt from experience.

Amy was like a mini doting mother to Steven. She copied everything I did and it was quite cute watching her. There was one funny incident, it wasn't at the time I hasten to add. We'd had given Amy a black toy horse which was named Blackie. Apt, I know. I was upstairs and Martin downstairs in the living room when all of a sudden we heard this almighty racket going down the stairs and a wail of Amy crying at the bottom of the stairs. As you can imagine both Martin and I shot out of the rooms we were in and ran to Amy. Amy was still holding onto the horse! We checked her over to make sure she had no broken bones and made sure that there was a gate placed there to stop her doing it again.

I was at home with two young children and was becoming bored. I tended to like a challenge. It was difficult to go out to work so I thought it would be easier to work from home. This was when I started up my own catering business. I ran that business for nine years and enjoyed every minute of it. It was hard work, don't think it wasn't, but I used to love the pleasure in making people happy by doing a good job and making their day special.

My first booking was special; you always remember the first in anything. I'd hired the staff, worked out what was needed for the function. My first function was a sit down three course meal. The girls wore black skirt, white blouse and white apron. It was a nerve wracking day making sure everything went right. The day ended and I was left with all the washing up! And one very happy bride and groom.

I don't know why I wanted to move again. The house we were living in was nice, it was a semi-detached with three bedrooms, the back garden had lots of fruit bushes and a couple of fruit trees, and we had a field behind the fence.

Because of that field we had extra visitors – mice! I don't mind them but when it came to them eating through packaging in the cupboards we had to do something about it; so we decided to go to the cat protection league to get a cat to ward off the mice. The cat didn't have a clue! It watched the mice running around and attacked baby Steven, so cat went back to the Cat's Protection post haste and we then got the council in to put down traps for them, we got rid of the mice eventually. It's really something when you get out the box of dry cat food and tip it out and out come baby mice! The box was being used as a nesting place.

We were on the move again, this time we moved to Twydall in Gillingham. I loved living in Twydall. We'd bought a double fronted semidetached ex council house that had loads of space and a garage out the back. Behind the house was a garage block where the kids used to play. We were close to local amenities with very good shops, it was ideal for me.

In that house we had many parties; family coming for dinner or tea, children's parties etcetera. In front of the house was a walkway and facing us were two schools, on the left was the junior school and on the right the infants, which was again ideal. Just around the corner was the playschool that the children used to attend.

I still continued to run my catering business and I expanded it to include a full wedding package such as car hire, photography, dress hire etc. I really enjoyed the work but it was hard. We'd spend the week from Thursday sorting out the venue's crockery and cutlery, making sure everything was in the trailer ready to be taken to the venue, the food list, buying, cooking, washing up, and repacking once we done the venue. The money I made from this once I'd paid the waitresses etc., paid for the 'extras', such as holidays. I used to say 'right, I've got two hundred pounds to spend on buying new clothes for you children', and out we used to go and have a very enjoyable day doing so.

On one occasion Martin and I went to Portugal for a holiday and left the children with their grandparents. We had a fantastic time there, but we brought an extra present back with us. I was pregnant again.

It was a surprise to the both of us as we'd decided that we had the two children, one of each. I do remember telling certain members of the family that I was expecting and their reaction was to get rid of it. I hasten to add it wasn't Martin who said this. I was shocked nevertheless. I don't believe that you should have an abortion just for the sake of it unless there is a threat to your own health or something seriously wrong with the baby. That's my belief, anyway.

Amy was seven and Steven was four when their baby brother was born. We named him Murrey. He was an absolute treasure. When he was born, Amy decided that she was going to be the mother. She was an absolute natural handling him, feeding him. It was like she had a live doll to play with. Martin's parents came up to visit us and said they would take Amy and Steven back home with them to Seaford in Sussex to allow us to spend time with the new baby. You should have heard Amy! She literally cried all the way to Sussex as she didn't want to leave her new brother and she thought that he would be grown up by the time she came back. Oh bless her.

When I think about Amy and Murrey, they have such a spiritual connection between them. It's as if they had a past life together as they are very close to each other. There is definitely a 'strong connection'.

When I was growing up, I seemed to try and find something that I belonged to by going to different churches. I went to the Salvation Army, Methodist, Church of England and some other churches. I just couldn't seem to settle into one church. Then I somehow got involved with the Born Again Christian movement. In some ways it resonated with me. We went to the local meetings every Sunday and I know the children hated it as they were so, so bored with just sitting there. I even decided to give my life to God and had the full immersion baptism, thinking this was going to absolutely change my life in some way. You guessed it, it didn't.

In some ways it was a little like brain washing. There were so many sins and Spiritualism was one of them. I had some tarot cards and I was made to burn them. That didn't make a difference to my life either. But, it was the beginning of me talking in 'Spirit tongue'. I will explain more about this later in the book.

I pulled away from the Born Again Christian movement after about seven years as I was becoming increasingly aware of the hypocrisy of some of the people. Don't get me wrong, there were some lovely church members there but I was looking beyond what they were preaching. I think I needed to experience this for what was to come up in the future. My mum, stepfather, sister and her husband all belonged to the movement.

One thing I did stipulate with regards to the children was the time they had to be in at night. They weren't allowed to be out on the streets late and if they were not in when I said they should be, they were not allowed out for every minute they were late. They therefore made sure they were in time. I was strict in many ways and I know they didn't like me for it. It was because I loved them so much that I didn't want anything or anyone to harm them. All the time I didn't realise that someone was harming someone very close to me and this hurt me deeply. If only I'd known sooner what was going on.

I became very worried about Amy as she seemed to be going further and further away from me. The change in her was very noticeable but I was so wrapped up with the business, running the house and looking after the children that I didn't think any more of it. I think she was about fourteen when she met the boyfriend who later became her husband.

My eldest son, Steven, was a very loving boy but he felt things deeply emotionally and always felt no one liked or loved him. He was also a very strong little man and I feel he's on a spiritual quest and that he is an old soul. My youngest son Murrey is such a character. He, I feel, has also been sent here for a reason. He is like a peace keeper, he is a deep thinker too. He likes to make people happy, he doesn't like seeing people down.

I don't know what got into me but the old itchy feet got to me again and after living in Twydall for nine years we were on the move again. If I'd known what the next 11 years was going to be like, I think we would have stayed where we were. Let's just say my life changed completely and it was hell.

CHAPTER 4

We moved to a four bedroomed house in Gillingham, Kent. (Have you noticed that our bedrooms are increasing with each move?) Poor Steven had to go to school in Twydall by bus; he was doing so well there. His eleven plus score was so high that the local grammar school was fighting to have him as a pupil. Amy moved closer to her secondary school; she only had to walk across and up the road. Murrey went to the local infants and then the juniors in Barnsole Road, Gillingham.

This house was a terraced house. You entered into the hall with the stairs going up on the right hand side, to the left was the living/dining room with a bar and from there you walked into the extension which had part of the kitchen and you walked around the corner and there was a galley type other kitchen. You could also get to the kitchen from the hall. There was three bedrooms on the first floor and up more stairs to the bedroom in the loft with a toilet en-suite. We did change the kitchen around and got rid of the galley part of the kitchen and turned it into an office.

We sorted out the house as it was in a filthy state and needed some work doing to it. I'm afraid Martin was a person who took a long time getting around to getting things done.

I noticed that my sight was deteriorating as I wasn't coping so well so I registered with Kent Association for the Blind and they gave me a white stick. It really hit home when I was handed and used the stick. I hated it, but needed it at the same time as I was walking into people and obstacles that were out of my range of sight.

One day, we were walking through Chatham High Street when Amy noticed a stall belonging to the Guide Dogs for the Blind and suggested I should go and find out about it. The thought of having a guide dog never occurred to me and the thought filled me with terror. It seemed as if I was having to admit that I needed help and to put my trust in an animal. It was saying I was failing as a person and branding myself as 'disabled'. With the deafness, no one could see I was wearing a hearing aid, but with a white stick or guide dog it was different.

It was the pity I couldn't cope with and not only that, the rudeness of people. I've had comments like 'you don't look blind'. People make it difficult for me which seems as if they are testing me to see if I really do have a sight problem. They'd talk to the person who was with me as if I wasn't there and didn't have a voice or was stupid. It's so frustrating and there have been many times that I've cried. My mum was with me on one occasion when we were in a supermarket checkout and the woman at the till kept turning to my mum, asking her the questions and not me. My mum bluntly told her that I had a brain and could answer for myself so why didn't she give it a go.

There were many things I missed with regards to how people were reacting towards me; it must have hurt my family so much to see such things. I know one thing; my children, despite what has happened in their lives, are fiercely protective of me if anyone has a go at me. Especially Amy; steer clear of her!

Back to the story. Someone from Guide Dogs came to visit me to assess my needs and concluded that, yes, I would benefit from having a guide dog and placed me on the waiting list. As it turned out, I only had to wait for a couple of months and I had my first guide dog called Samba.

Samba was a yellow Labrador aged five who unfortunately was handed back to Guide Dogs because his previous owner became ill and was unable to continue having him. When we were introduced for the first time, he took to me straight away. He came and placed his paw on me and that was it. I had to go away for two weeks to train with him, learning to trust that he would stop at kerbs and not walk out into the road. It was really difficult to let go and place your total trust in an animal. I qualified with Samba on my birthday, 18th July, which was a good reason to have a double celebration.

The family used to find it frustrating when we were all walking through a crowded High Street. I would be walking with Samba on harness and the family would be walking beside me. When people used to see me with my guide dog they use to part like the Red Sea before the Israelites! They then closed in behind me, leaving them stranded. They used to shout 'hey, we're with her!' to the passers-by.

In 1994, my life was going to change again. This was the time when Spiritualism came into my life in a big way and turned my life upside down.

It was 1st August 1994. Steven and I walked to our local shops to buy groceries and he was complaining of back pains and I said that he was to take it easy when we got back home. When we stepped back into the house, Steven cried out with the severe pain he was getting to his back and collapsed onto the floor and couldn't move. I panicked a bit and immediately phoned for the doctor who said I was to stay with Steven and he was going to call for an ambulance for him. We were at Medway hospital for some hours before we were seen but eventually they admitted him onto the children's ward. I was absolutely beside myself with worry wondering what was happening to him. What made the waiting even worse was the hospital's practice of rotating the staff dealing with Steven's case to other duties every twelve months, which meant that the new team seemingly had to start at square one every time they took over.

Steven was in hospital for six weeks. They ran tests after tests and tried to get him to stand and he just cried out with the pain in his back whenever he put his feet to the floor. He hated the hospital food and refused to eat it which worried the Ward Sister so much that she called the hospital chef for help to ask him if he would cook Steven a beef burger in a bun. Not only did he do it, he actually brought the burger up himself. The Ward Sister was amazed because the kitchen staff had never put themselves out like that before.

There were times when I slept in the ward to be with Steven at night to keep him company. There were stories of things he got up to, one of which was having wheelchair races around the ward and getting up to all sorts. The doctors could not find the cause of his problems. They even suggested that things were not right at home and that he was putting it on. I was furious at this suggestion because everything was okay at home and in any case why would he want to spend six weeks of the school summer holidays in hospital?

We were able to take Steven out in a wheelchair at weekends to give him a break from the hospital. It was on one of these occasions that we met Stevens's best friend at a boot fair. He promptly went home and told his mother about the news and she later phoned me to ask if it would be possible to come and see him. Tommy's mother, Jennifer, used to be a nurse.

Jennifer and I seem to hit it off straight away. She later confessed to me that she thought I wouldn't want to know her because she felt that I was classier than her. It was the first time I had come into contact with someone to do with Spiritualism. I was talking to her one day about my eyes and my efforts to trace my father; she told me not to bother as he had passed to Spirit. I was shocked by her comments and thought she was nuts.

After six weeks of running all the tests and coming up with no reasons as to why Steven should be unable to walk, the doctors decided to discharge him. Even after the six weeks he could barely walk around. It was a few days after coming home from hospital that he tripped on a mat in the lounge and fell. It was in falling that somehow his back just went click into place and he was able to walk again. We were all so relieved and happy that he was able to walk and was on the mend.

Jennifer suggested going to a Spiritualist church but she said I wasn't to tell Martin as she felt that he would be unhappy with the idea. We found a church in Chatham called The Sanctuary of Healing. When I walked into the church I felt that I'd come home. It was the final piece of a jigsaw in searching for a place to belong, something that had been lacking in my life for some time.

After a short while of disappearing with Jennifer in going to the meetings at the church that I finally told Martin. Martin was very relieved as he thought I was having an affair and that Jennifer was taking me to meet 'the other man'. On the evening I told Martin, he hugged me and then turned on the television. In a shocked voice he said that, while the credits were rolling at the end of a programme, the screen had changed colour and the name Vera had appeared. He didn't believe what he was seeing, so he blinked his eyes and the name disappeared.

Vera was a very special person. She was the mother of Danny who was Martin's best friend. Before the children came along, we all used to go camping and have a fantastic time with sharing and laughter. She was a wonderful kind-hearted person, and I felt she was like a second mother to me. You could talk to her about anything and she had an open house where anyone could drop by. It was a tragedy when she died after going into hospital for a routine operation. She was young and it should never have happened.

I was only just coming into Spiritualism and trying to understand what it was about. I felt Jennifer was manipulating me a little bit as she kept saying that she was in constant contact with my father who had passed to Spirit and I couldn't understand why he wasn't talking to me. She had a friend who happened to have a particular ornament of an owl. She told me that my father used to love owls and said it would help me to get closer to him if I would buy it. She asked for sixty pounds for it and I paid up like a stupid idiot.

I later found out that Jennifer and her friend were addicted to prescription drugs and were using that money to buy more. I was so angry and disappointed that a 'friend' would do such a thing. It shows when you first come into Spiritualism you are vulnerable to people who know of your weakness when you are desperate to find out about your loved-one in spirit, it's a cruel thing to do to anybody. I suppose I was feeling jealous if I'm to be honest. Jennifer was saying that if I was to buy this particular ornament or listen to this particular song I would get closer to him. I never felt any connection with him. I was as gullible as I was desperate to connect with a father I never knew and to find out more about him.

Since I joined and became involved in the Spiritualist Church, we started to become aware of spiritual activity in the house in Gillingham. Keys would be moved, and there were footsteps in the room above when I was alone in the house. Amy's boyfriend, Mason, used to stay at times and sleep on her bedroom floor. On this particular night she felt a presence standing above them and that Mason was being attacked by an entity. This obviously scared her to bits. Amy also used to be lying in her bed and feel someone sitting on the end of her bed. She'd open her eyes and see a little blond haired girl just looking at her and not saying a word. There were times when Amy would run the bath water and go back into her room whilst the bath was filling up. When she went back into the bathroom the tap would be turned off.

As you can imagine this scared the life out of Amy so I decided to get someone in to move the spirit on and cleanse the house. After that; the activity did stop; for a while. Then one day, after a few months had passed, a spirit entity attacked Amy's boyfriend. They saw he was man wearing a hat and a trench coat. We had not mentioned anything about what was happening to our neighbour next door but when I happened to mention this incident to her she was shocked because she too was having a problem with a spirit in her bedroom. This was next to Amy's room and the spirit used to pass from one house to the other. She said that she used to find her pillows had been moved and other things were happening. I'm wondering now if it was because I'd become spiritually aware that he was trying to get through to me and I sent him away, or did I?

Whilst all of the spiritual activity was going on, Amy became ill. She was passing out at school, having severe pains in her stomach and I was taking her to the doctors and they kept sending her away saying there was absolutely nothing wrong with her. She was still suffering though. It was when she had another stomach attack that I had to do something about it. I didn't want to go back to the doctors so I took her straight to the hospital. I got the same response as from the doctors; no answers. I became frantic with worry as I couldn't bear to watch my little girl suffering; I even took her to another hospital hoping we'd get some answers but, again, they came up with nothing.

We were desperate to find out the cause of Amy's illness. It was whilst I talking to Steven's football coach about Amy that he told me about his next door neighbour; that she was a Kinesiologist and might be able to help. I'd never heard of such a thing but was desperate to get some help for Amy. When I told Amy of where we were going she said 'she won't tell you anything that I don't want you to know will she'? I did wonder why she would say such a thing and I assured her that everything would be done in confidence and I wouldn't question what Helen had found.

Amy was bent double with pain when we arrived at the Kinesiologist's counselling room but when we left an hour later, she walked out upright. I didn't question what the practitioner was doing as it had worked as far as I was concerned. Kinesiology is quite fascinating and it's amazing what they can find out about your body and state of mind. They do muscle testing using certain objects containing chemicals to find out what your body is lacking. They also work with crystals to get the balance of the energy right for the body and the surrounding environment. They can detect Ley Lines that may be causing a lot of negativity. The subject is endless but very effective. Money was no object if it meant Amy was not going to suffer anymore.

It turned out that Amy was suffering from stomach migraine, something that I've never heard of as I thought you had migraine of the head. This was caused by a build-up of stress and worry. I didn't know why Amy should have been suffering from this. After she had the treatment, she was able to go back to school and didn't suffer with her stomach area. It was after Amy had her last treatment when Helen, the Kinesiologist turned to me and said that there was something deep within Amy that was bothering her and that she couldn't get to the root of what it was. I was a little disturbed by this comment and could not think of anything that could be upsetting her.

It was all happening to Amy when I'd hit upon the idea of opening a cake and bread shop as I'd noticed that there wasn't one around where we were living, and I missed the former bakery that was available in Twydall. There was, however, an empty wool shop on the corner of Fourth Avenue leading into Sturdee Avenue in Gillingham which needed a lot of work doing to it. We had to rewire it and add plug sockets and so on.

I didn't know where to start looking for shop fittings so we went and bought kitchen units and worktops. We didn't start with the café; that was added later.

It took my business partner and me a long time to try and think of a name for the shop and I had an inspiration to call it 'Fallen Angels'. Fallen Angels I hear you say; the reason behind the name was a suggestion that you were innocent until you tried one of our cakes or sandwiches.

My business partner was a friend of mine and we were just sorting out the partnership agreement when she decided to pull out of the business and demanded all of her money back. Her reason for pulling out was that she wasn't getting any money out of it. We'd had only been open for five weeks and I was left alone to run the business as I couldn't get out of the lease. If only she'd stayed because it became successful. I started just selling bread and cakes and then I decided to sell sandwiches and rolls made from uncut bread. We were having queues out of the door. I then extended the business by adding a café. It was hard work and made very little money after paying the staff wages. There were times when I cried with the exhaustion and worry of wondering how I was going to pay the bills. On top of all this, I still had a home to run and children to sort out. Bless them, they were not having a good time of it. The only thing they enjoyed was the left over cakes although after a while they even got fed up with that!

We'd opened the shop and in the January/February of 1995. Steven was sent home from school with severe pains to his side. He was laying on the settee with a raging temperature and once again we phoned the doctors, explained Steven's condition and they said we were to phone for an ambulance straight away. He was taken down to theatre more or less straight away as he had severe appendicitis. It was awful watching him go through the theatre doors, you feel so helpless, I left there crying and when we was in the waiting room

Martin just went to sleep. I could have slapped him! Stevens's operation was a little complicated as his appendix had got wrapped around his rib cage which is much higher up than it should be.

It was especially hard when it came to our first Christmas after opening the shop. We just did not have any money. I could say it was a worry. How were we going to afford the presents and food? Mum came to the rescue. We had the basics of everything and I bought the presents from a charity shop. I know some people will knock the charity shops, but they have been a God-send as far as I was concerned. I will say, we did have a great Christmas in the end.

We also used to get a lot of spiritual activities in the shop. These are just some of the things 'Spirit' used to do. I established that one particular entity was a man and that Amy was also very aware of him. There was a time when I was sorting out a customer's order for a birthday cake. I was standing next to the cash register, but not touching it, when the 'till' opened all by itself, not once, but twice. The look on the customers face was a picture. I just brushed it off by saying that the till had a mind of its own. The male entity used to turn the radio up or off if I was alone in the shop or move utensils out of Amy's reach when she was cooking and she used to get mad especially when it was very busy in the shop. The roller blinds had long cords which you pulled to open or close the blinds. The Spirit used to pull these away from the window horizontal; now that was scary. These are just a few of the things the entity did. I did manage to tune into him and found out his name was Robert Green and that he was a wealthy ship owner. He said that he was wrongfully hanged for something he didn't do. I also used to write poems and do automatic handwriting, and he used to come through and tell me stories. I found it fascinating. I loved working with spirit and I wanted to learn more and more.

One of the things you may notice once you become aware of Spirit around you is how you have a thirst for knowledge about the subject. There is a feeling of going around in circles because you don't know where to start, who to ask the questions, where to go. It can be frightening for some, I was lucky as I seemed to just take it in my stride, the feeling of 'knowing' that I was safe. It's when you begin to think about Spirit and your journey that you begin to notice certain people come into your life to help or guide you. Or you see a sign, it could be anything, which you cannot ignore because the meaning is all at once very clear to you. I wasn't aware of Spiritualist churches or about New Age as I'd never heard of it.

I met a lot of people in the shop and there used to be a man who would come in wearing nothing on his feet, only socks. He was a driving instructor and when he was driving past the shop, he'd come in to get a Cornish pasty. Mind you, it had to be very well baked to the point of nearly being burnt. I was also noticing that he was coming into the shop quite regularly and we'd strike up a conversation about different things. He also used to do body massage as well as Swedish massage which is a deep muscle massage. Because I'd been going through a lot, I thought it would be nice to have one and he was shocked when I told him that I would be bringing Samba as he had no idea that I had a sight problem. His name was Charles.

I was attending church regularly every week and sometimes Martin used to come with me. I wasn't too sure if it was something he was really interested in. I'd receive messages from the Medium on the rostrum and they used to bring my father forward. From the information they gave me I managed to piece together some ideas about my father. They also suggested that I should join a circle to develop my spiritual gifts. This was news to me as I wasn't aware I had any 'gifts'. After a while I did join a circle which was being run by a man called Richard. Richard was to play a very big part in my life years later.

We used to meet once a week on a Monday in the church vestry, there was a group of about six of us. We had to learn how to say a prayer asking for protection, do a meditation and then we did exercises in connecting with Spirit and give messages etc. We also used different tools like drawing, tarot cards, writing; the list is endless. There was one occasion whilst in meditation when I distinctly heard a door opening from my right hand side and someone walking past me and opening the door at the other side of the room. The door handle sounded like an old fashioned round type where you had to turn a knob to open the door but when I looked at the doors they had modern straight handles. I asked if someone had come into the room whilst we were meditating and the answer was no one had entered.

I had noticed over a period of time that Amy wasn't happy so I thought of an idea that would please her. Amy had a big interest in The Clothes Show and there was an exhibition in Manchester. I thought it would be a lovely idea to take Amy to the exhibition; just the two of us having some quality mum and daughter time together. We had a great but exhausting day. It was on the next day when a thought kept going through my head. Eventually I called Amy to the kitchen where I was preparing our evening meal. It took a lot of courage for me to ask Amy what was the matter and when she told me and who was involved I was in shock. I've spoken to Amy about this and she had asked me not to go into details here as she feels that no good purpose would be served by dragging the incident up again. Suffice it to say, her revelation rocked the family and we were never to be the same again.

What hurt me so much was that I didn't see what was happening and I failed Amy in not keeping my promise when she was born to protect her. This situation destroyed the relationship between my mother and myself as I wouldn't talk to her for some time because the one person who caused all the trouble was her husband and she stuck by him, putting her needs before her daughter and granddaughter. Her husband Henry pleaded guilty to what he'd done and got two years suspended sentence. I know this is unspiritual of me, but Henry died of leukaemia a year after the court case and I was glad, God forgive me.

It was during this time I'd never felt so alone. I was watching my family falling apart as we were all hurting in different ways. It also felt as if it was our fault that we spoke up and did something about it. If you were to ask me would I go through it again, I would say yes because as far as I was concerned I wanted justice for my daughter, justice that I never got.

Eventually after a long while, Mum contacted me and asked that we met somewhere so that we could talk, to which I agreed. She put her side of the story to me and asked for my forgiveness. In some ways I did but nothing was ever the same again between us. We had such a strong family unit before all this happened, big family get-togethers, Christmases, parties; that had all changed.

I was having further problems with my eyes. They were not as clear as they used to be so I went to the hospital and the consultant said I had cataracts in both eyes and suggested I had them removed. I had one cataract removed and was scheduled to have the other one done. I went into hospital in Maidstone to have the second eye done and all seemed well. It was within a few days of being discharged that my eye wasn't feeling right. It became very sore and I went to the eye emergency department. I was admitted into hospital straight away. In the emergency department they had to inject morphine just below my eye and a very strong anti-biotic and admitted me into hospital. I was very frightened indeed. They had me in a room of my own and I had to have these drops placed into my eyes hourly, day and night. I was so tired that I cried and begged them to let me sleep and my eye was so sore with the continuous drops being put in.

I was taken down into theatre to have the eye looked at to discover what was going on. If ever you want to know what a numb skull is like, it's weird. I had numbing injections all around the eye as I was awake throughout the operation. They took my eye out and I saw multi-colours flashing around but I just wanted to be put to sleep whilst they were investigating. The doctors couldn't work out what was going on so they referred me to St. Thomas's Hospital in London to undergo further investigations.

I was in St Thomas's for a week. Whilst I was in hospital in Maidstone and London, I'd been doing a lot of thinking and writing a journal, trying to make sense of what I was feeling. What I felt was that Martin and I were drifting apart. We were not the same anymore and I began to notice things. I guess I had fallen out of love. Because

I was so young, I didn't have the experience of life by going on holidays with other girls; going to night clubs, all the usual things you did when you were experiencing life. I went straight into a serious relationship and knew nothing else. Don't get me wrong, Martin was a hardworking man. He was good and kind but something had gone and I noticed it when Amy was going through her trouble. It was something he'd said to me when I told him about Amy that caused the light in me to go out and I began to question everything. I was very lonely during that time too, we just didn't talk and that made it worse. It was my fault as well, I just didn't know how to talk either. My fear was kicking in again because at the back of my mind was the thought that, if I was to say anything what was going to happen to me.

One day whilst at the hospital in London, Martin and I went outside for a bit. We were standing facing Westminster and I told Martin that I wasn't happy and that things had to change if we were to make our marriage work. He agreed, but with Martin, nothing ever lasted for long.

Eventually I was discharged from the hospital in London. They couldn't find out what was going on either. But I did end up having double vision for which they referred me back to Maidstone Eye Hospital to have eye tests to have glasses with prisms in the lenses. When I went for the tests, there was nothing they could do for me. They suggested that I wore a patch over the eye and just got on with it. I was not a happy bunny.

Life returned to some sort of normality once I got back home. Martin hadn't really changed after our talk. I was still having to sort out all the everyday bills etc. Charles was still coming into the shop and he already knew about my operations and realised that I was feeling rather low so he suggested that it would be nice if I was to accompany him to a ladies night at his Masonic club. I'd never heard of Freemasons. I asked Martin if this was okay with him and he said yes. I did have a fabulous evening, it was really lovely dressing up as it was a bow tie and long dress function. Charles made me feel quite special and I suppose I was looking for somebody to take me away from all the struggles I was going through. I was also starting to have feelings for him; he was a real charmer of a man, if only I looked away.

During this time, poor Murrey kept coming up into our bedroom and sleeping on our bedroom floor. We couldn't understand why he should be wanting to do this when he had a bedroom of his own. What we didn't know was he was experiencing nasty things with Spirit activity and he was also sensing something was wrong between Martin and myself. It was his way of trying to stop what was going to happen next.

I'd decided that I couldn't go on with Martin. I'd got to the point when I was asking God not to let me wake up the next day. I just couldn't take any more of the unhappiness I was feeling inside. It was with a heavy heart that I made the decision, went to speak to Mum about it telling her what I was going through as I asked for my mum's blessing which she gave me, and I also spoke to a Minister at the Spiritualist Church about what I was going through. I knew that what I was about to do was not going to be easy. Our marriage was over. Despite what people thought at the time I did not leave Martin for Charles. It was the furthest thing on my mind.

Leaving was one of the worst things I have had to do. Firstly I told Martin our marriage was over and then we sat the children down and told them. I will never forget that moment. I'd hurt my family deeply, but I knew there was no going back.

CHAPTER 5

I moved out of our marital home in January 1997. Martin and I asked the children who they would like to live with. Poor Murrey didn't have a choice as there wasn't anyone to look after him during the day. Amy and Steven were old enough to look after themselves whilst Martin was at work. Murrey and I moved into a furnished house in Sittingbourne. If I'd been clearer thinking, I should have stopped Jennifer from taking over and persuading me to move closer to her. Jennifer could be quite a persuasive and manipulative person which I hadn't realised at the time

The first night on sleeping at the new house was quite scary. At about eleven p.m. in the evening, my bed and the picture on the wall started to shake and I could hear this deep rumble in the distance, it got closer and closer and the bed shook more, then the train went past. What I didn't know was that there was a main line rail track just yards away from the house. This disturbance used to happen every night, but I got quite used to it and you could nearly set your watch by the train time.

I was so guilty and suffering with depression due to my actions that I had caused to the family a lot of distress. There were times when I wanted to end it all. The rail track was so close that I thought of just ending my life, I just didn't want the pain anymore. Another option I thought about was turning to drink as a way of blotting out the emotional pain. However, I didn't go down that route either thank goodness, as I could have become an alcoholic. There was something very strong inside of me that stopped me from doing this. I know my family thought I didn't care about them or anything else and thought I was being very selfish, if only they knew.

Murrey lived with me during the week and went home to Martin at weekends. I'd have the whole family together on a Sunday for Sunday roast and we'd go out for a walk or drive. During this time, I began to think about my marriage and thought that maybe I'd made a mistake. Charles was popping by more and more. Had I not been so worried about what was going on around me, I would have felt what my guides were trying to tell me. They were trying to warn me to keep away from him, but I wasn't listening. A hard lesson to learn. Charles was such a charming man, took me out and showed me a different lifestyle to what I was used to.

Having said all of that, I wanted to give my marriage to Martin another go. There was a condition; I was going to stay where I was living and he had to prove himself to me by taking over the responsibility for sorting out the household bills etc. and we were going to start a new life by moving to a new area and going for a pub with a restaurant. I asked Martin to make a start and after a couple of weeks nothing was happening. Then one day Martin turned to me and said 'Ang, can you sort this out'. I knew then that he would never change, and I told him again that our marriage was over. This really turned the whole family against me as I'd given them hope that we would all be together again, but I just knew I couldn't go backwards as it took two people to work on a relationship. I never told the children the real reasons, I took all the blame as I didn't want them to lose the respect they had for their father. I became the outcast of the family, and everyone gathered around and supported Martin. They didn't know the real reasons for the break-up. There was only one person who did, that was Mum. She knew more than she let on.

Charles and I started to see each other more often and I introduced him to Mum she took an instant dislike to him as she felt he was looking down his nose at our family. Mum felt that he was just tolerating her just to please me and that my family were beneath him. Charles made her feel very uncomfortable and it was many years later when she told me about how she felt about him.

Martin was still coming to the house in Sittingbourne. This really annoyed Charles as he wanted Martin out of my life. Then one day I received a phone call to say that Martin had been in an accident in his lorry. He'd crashed into the back of a slow moving crane and in doing so the lorry he was driving tipped over onto its side. He was very lucky that he wasn't severely injured or killed. I had Martin stay at my house in Sittingbourne to look after him as there was no one else to do so. We did do some talking but something inside of me told me not to go back.

Charles proved to be quite manipulative; it was May of 1997 when Charles knocked on my door and said that he'd been thrown out of the house he was sharing with his ex-partner. He had nowhere to live and supposedly had slept in his car for one night and at a friend's house another. I later found out the real truth; it was all lies. He wanted to move in with me so that he could stop Martin from being with me and his ex-partner hadn't thrown him out. The reason I know this was she told me when later we became good friends. Charles had also made her life a misery over the years. Charles and Cheryl had moved in together and after a short while, they decided to live separate lives in separate bedrooms. I said Charles could stay but that he had to sleep on the sofa. I had my son with me and it wasn't right he should be seeing another man moving in and feeling that I was replacing Murrey's dad.

I was travelling back to Gillingham to run the business and Martin was also helping out as he was off work for a while. It was during this time that I had to sell the business as we couldn't keep going on the way we were. Charles was also saying he didn't want to live in Gillingham or to be involved in the business so I sold it to one of the ladies who worked for me. I was sad to let the business go as it could have been really successful but once again I had to stop something I loved and hand it onto someone else. The whole reason why I started the business was to try and improve our lives as we were struggling on the wages that Martin was earning. I also felt humiliated by having a disability. I was told by the job centre to simply continue drawing my disability benefits. Thinking back I was always shunned and made to feel useless but I felt that I had something to prove. However, this all proved very costly in the end because I lost my children, whom I loved dearly but didn't know how to show it.

I was still going to my spiritualist church in Chatham and receiving healing for my eye. It was on a Monday in June of 1997 when I went for my normal healing after I'd been to my circle. Whilst I was laying on the healing couch with my eyes closed I began to see visions of a man who looked like a witch doctor and during this time I felt a warm lovely feeling around my head. I mentioned this to the healer and he confirmed it was his guide that worked with him during the healing. I didn't think any more about the healing that evening.

It was the next day when I was alone in the house doing the housework. The sun was shining and I suddenly realised that I could see properly; the blurriness and double vision had gone. I was so happy but scared at the same time as I thought it would be short lived. Charles came home that evening and I couldn't stop him from talking so much about himself and his day. When I finally managed to butt in and told him of my news, he didn't show much emotion about this good news. However, I know the rest of the family were happy for me.

Charles asked me to marry him later that year and I said yes; why I will never know. I think I was afraid of him a bit and didn't know what to do. As usual I just went along with everything that was going on around me. Martin and I were divorced in November and a couple of weeks later Charles and I were married. Quick I know. It really was a sad day for me as I knew deep down I was making a big mistake. We decided to get married at The Shurland in Eastchurch on the Isle of Sheppey. We'd booked a room so that we could all get ready, have my make-up done and Jennifer was supposed to be helping us all but she kept disappearing to go and have a fag and she was going through another crisis of her own. Murrey was my page boy and I was so hoping that Amy and Steven would come to the wedding, I kept looking out of the window of the bedroom but they never turned up nor did I hear from them. Charles was shocked when he saw me for the first time as he didn't have a clue to what I would be wearing, I wore an ivory wedding dress with a lovely head dress to match. How can I explain about my wedding day, all I can say I felt detached, it was someone else getting married not me.

On our wedding day, my brother wanted to knock Charles' block off. During the main speeches Charles never once referred to me, complimented me, said how happy he was, the happiest day etc. He made a speech to his ex-partner saying what a wonderful person she was, and presented her with a birthday cake. I should have known that from that day onwards there would always be three people in our marriage.

Charles spent most of his time at the wedding reception away from me flirting with a young girl that was young enough to be his daughter. To tell you how bad it was, his ex-partner Cheryl had a go at him and told him to behave himself. The rest of my family were not impressed with him; they just didn't like him at all. I didn't even get to have our first dance alone together. Charles got his step-son to dance with us; I will mention here that his step-son was starved of oxygen when he was born and consequently was brain damaged. His step-son also came before everything and there were times when I saw Charles ill-treating him.

Charles and I spent our honeymoon on a coach trip in Scotland. It was the other members on the trip that made our honeymoon as Charles knew nearly all of them as they all came from Isle of Sheppey. It was on the morning of us going away on our honeymoon that Charles had a go at me for turning on the lights bearing in mind it was dark and I couldn't see. I just couldn't see he was playing with my mind. Mum could. On the coach trip we stopped at Gretna Green and had our marriage blessed over an anvil and received a certificate to say so.

There was one funny incident whilst on honeymoon. After a tiring day of travelling around Scotland, we'd gone up to bed. We'd got into our night attire and tried to get into our bed, to no avail. We just couldn't seem to make sense of what had happened to our bedding. Eventually we sorted it out by stripping the bed and remaking it. We went down to breakfast the next morning and the rest of the coach company were all watching us, sniggering and laughing at us. They'd had a talk to the hotel staff and asked for our room key and 'apple pied' our bedding. We really had a good laugh about it.

We had got back from the honeymoon and started to settle into a routine. Charles was a driving instructor and also did the odd massage treatment here and there. Charles also told me that he was not prepared to pay rent for the house we were living in and he wanted to get back to his beloved island; his words not mine. I didn't have a choice in the matter as I couldn't afford to pay the rent myself as all benefits had been stopped.

It was now close to our first Christmas as a married couple and I was a great believer in making Christmas special, having a tree and decorations etc. However, Charles turned to me and said he didn't want anything to do with Christmas and was not prepared to help me to sort it out or to pay for it. Would you believe it, it was Martin who bought me a small tree with lights etc. He said he was doing it for his son but I was very grateful to him all the same. Murrey went home to his father's for Christmas; I was sad that he went and not seeing Amy and Steven but at the same time; happy because Murrey wouldn't have to endure the terrible Christmas I had.

I became very ill with a severe migraine, the worst I have ever known it. I spent all of my Christmas lying on the settee, I just couldn't get my head off the pillow. It was so bad that I had an emergency appointment with the doctor and she told me that I was suffering with severe stress.

Life was about to get even worse.

Charles had a friend who was in the building trade amongst other things. His friend had bought a derelict house where an old man had died. His friend offered Charles the use of the house and warned him that the workmen would be going in to refurbish it. When I saw the house for the first time, I really cried. I just couldn't believe what I was going into. I was going backwards not forward. Charles turned on me and told me to pull myself together; we were going to be living there. We moved in in January 1998.

Charles had told me that I was responsible for paying for anything that Murrey needed. He wanted nothing to do with him. Charles was hoping that Murrey would move back in with his father. Don't get me wrong, Charles never ever laid a finger on Murrey but he did make his life very uncomfortable. I can hear you all saying, why did you put up with it? But when you live with someone who plays mind games with you, it's very difficult to leave. This also triggered all the emotions from what my step father Eric had done, although I wasn't aware of this for years. Everything that happens to you goes into your sub-conscious mind and stays there. All it takes is an action, a word or something you see to trigger those emotions or memories. It may be something that happened years ago and you had forgotten it but your sub-conscious mind never forgets.

When I think about Murrey and what he had endured, he is one very special boy. He was a tower of strength to me, he could have said that he wanted to go and live with his father but he didn't. I do know that Murrey suffered in some way mentally. Sometimes things come out in conversation about how Murrey was feeling and the tears he had shed, he never once told me himself. He was my rock and if Charles started on him I turned on Charles straight away. This is something Charles hated. He hated not being the number one, not being put first. I'm sorry, he's my flesh and blood and I love him dearly.

Our living conditions were as follows. The whole house was bare wooden flooring; no carpets anywhere. The curtains were the original ones. We had to borrow three armchairs for somewhere to sit and the television was sitting on a cardboard box that had stuff inside of it. I had a table to prepare our food on as there was only a sink with one tap in the kitchen. Upstairs in the bathroom there was only the toilet and nothing else. We had a put you up bed settee with a foam mattress of two inches to sleep on and Murrey had a camp bed. That was it.

We had to go out every day to a café for dinner and a launderette to do our washing. I didn't know this at the time, but Murrey was so cold that he used to go downstairs and get Samba to take him back upstairs so that he had him lay beside him to keep him warm. Murrey never told me he was cold, otherwise I would have done something for him. He only had a sleeping bag.

Poor Samba. My guide dog was also suffering as Charles didn't want him there either. We also had 'extra visitors' from the world of spirit; staying with us. I'm not sure if they were there to protect Murrey and myself, because Charles and Murrey used to see them. There was one occasion when I was sitting downstairs and I distinctly felt someone sit down beside me and I shot upstairs to tell Charles about it. By this time we had a bath and Charles was in it. He looked at me and said 'yes I know about the spirit'. I asked him how he knew and he replied, 'He's standing right next to you'. By the way Charles was describing the spirit entity it was sounding like my real father. He was there beside me all the time.

Charles' work was all over the place, trying to juggle his driving, which was declining, and the massage work. I suggested that he should start his own massage business and rent a room. Eventually he did and opened up his own deep massage treatment business and ended the driving school. I also complimented the business by training as a reflexologist and in Indian head massage treatments. I worked hard on the business, making sure someone was at the premises at all times, taking calls and making the bookings. Charles always seems to be swanning around the town or going to different places and not taking much interest in the business. He just didn't have the business sense.

It was in January of 1998 when I went to the local Spiritualist church in Sheerness. I used to take Murrey with me, as it was better than being at the dump we were living in. I really enjoyed going there every week, as they made you feel very welcomed. It was at this church a few years later when I demonstrated my mediumship by taking a Sunday service. I will tell you more about that later.

My mum and family were very worried about Murrey and me. When they saw the conditions I was living in, Mum absolutely flew at Charles. Mum was never backwards in coming forward when she was upset. This was something I never saw personally as it was the family who told me what she had said years later. Just let say she was not a happy bunny, it must have stirred up memories for her too and she couldn't believe that I was going through the self-same things that she had endured previously.

We lived in this dump for a while and eventually mine and Charles money came through from my divorce and Cheryl buying out Charles half of the house they had shared. Charles was at it again, making decisions about where we were to live. He decided to buy a bungalow (shack) in Minster on the Isle of Sheppey which measured fifteen feet by twenty two feet total with a lean to housing the kitchen of a sort. The floor in the kitchen had a hole in it. It consisted of a living room through to another room and off that was the bathroom with the lean to. He replaced the bathroom suite and moved the door from the front to the side of the building. From this he made a tiny room for Murrey's bedroom and he was squeezed into there. Again Charles wasted money by not completing anything.

We were sleeping in the front room and we turned the back room into a living room of sorts. There were boxes and our possessions all stacked up as we had nowhere to store them. We had planning permission to build and extend it, but after Charles got the quote, he refused to take out a small mortgage to complete the work. It was diabolical living there too. So much so that I had to make a heart breaking decision to rehouse Samba. It wasn't fair on him as he wasn't allowed to move around and Charles wouldn't let me take him out on harness to work him. Charles wanted to take control of everything. I'm happy to say that Jennifer took Samba in and he lived a very happy life until he crossed the rainbow bridge.

The stress I was going through was so severe that one day I couldn't go out of the house. I began to panic but in the end I had to force myself to get out of the door. It was in this house that I began to suffer with panic attacks. I was asleep one night, Murrey was in the other room and all of a sudden I woke up, I had a feeling of not being able to breathe, shaking, I thought I must get myself out of this off whatever it is happening so I asked Charles to talk to me. He sort of did but it wasn't working so I begged him to phone for an ambulance as I really couldn't breathe. They came and took me to hospital and Charles just went back to bed. At the hospital they told me of what I was suffering and then said I could go home. How could I when there was no one there to take me and I was in my night attire? The one person I could think of was Martin and I called him, said if I was to pay him petrol money would he be able to get me home. To my relief he agreed. The panic attacks lasted for nine years when I eventually managed to overcome them.

At this bungalow, we had a lot of Spiritual happenings. I also feel that we had the same Spirit that was at the first house by the way Charles was describing him. Murrey too continued to see Spirits, even sitting on the bottom of his bed. I really do believe that we were being looked after thinking about it now. Charles also used to see monks walking past the window and they smiled at him. Where we were living, there was an Abbey close by and the grounds where our bungalow was situated used to be kept by monks.

We were on the move yet again. This time Charles had decided, without my knowing it, to buy a thirty-five foot caravan on a caravan site that belonged to his friend. His reasons for this were that he had suffered five bouts of pneumonia and needed to get out of the conditions we were living in. It wouldn't have been like that if he'd got his finger out and sorted out the house. Murrey was also really suffering and he never told me what was going on with him, he just kept it quite. We did use to do sneaky things and enjoy ourselves when Charles wasn't around but somehow Charles always found out and made me pay the price. He was very good at playing mental games was our Charles.

We moved into this caravan which had one double bedroom and one single bedroom that had a bunk bed. You could just about get into this room. The rest of the caravan was open plan, the kitchen had a two ring cooker and grill, but no oven. The seating was very uncomfortable as it was under the windows. The only saving grace about living there was the view from the window. This looked out over the sea and the sunsets were beautiful. There were a lot of Spiritual activities on that site which had a ley line running through it. Charles was walking around the park one night and he came home scared as he felt he was surrounded by presences. I went with him one night to feel for myself but I didn't feel a thing.

Murrey began to see a lot more Spirits. He even saw Vikings marching towards him, a lady wearing a Victorian gown on the cliff top looking out to sea, and she turned to him and smiled. It was like he was being protected too.

Whilst we were living here I became a grandmother for the first time. Amy had given birth to a gorgeous baby boy who arrived ten weeks early in April 1999. She named him Jamie. He did struggle at first and wouldn't let go of the oxygen tank to breathe on his own at first but eventually he did. I have a picture taken of Amy holding Jamie where there is a white cord linking Amy to Jamie and coming out to me. I'm happy to say that Jamie is now a strapping lad of six feet three inches; he towers above me. Again Charles wanted to take over. He loves babies and young children, and this is a rare occasion when you see the soft side of him; then the brick wall goes up.

I was so unhappy living on the caravan site. I just couldn't take anymore as I was becoming more and more isolated. Charles had total control as I couldn't go anywhere without him and there was nowhere to go. I'd decided that I was going to leave him. I'd got Jennifer to help me find a house in Sittingbourne and was going to move into it once I had my hysterectomy operation. I made all the arrangements from the phone box on the site when Charles wasn't around. The plan was that I was going to stay with Mum in Gravesend when I had my operation to recover and then tell him I wasn't going back.

Let's just say I upset and let so many people down. I did tell Charles that I wasn't going back to him and as you can imagine he kept ringing me, crying down the phone, saying he would change and to give him another chance and I did. There was one condition, he would not pick me up from Mum's, and I had to make my own way back to him. I can hear you all shouting 'WHY'? Indeed why. My hormones were all over the place and I wasn't thinking straight, I really thought he would change; big mistake. Does this remind you of someone? My mum did the self-same thing and I was following in her footsteps.

Charles really punished me. He was hard as nails when I was crying. He wanted to know why I'd left and I told him. I will never forget the look on his face. There was no emotion there. He also left me for a week in the caravan on my own with no food and I had to try and walk to the shops and get some as I was not allowed to lift or do anything. I just couldn't tell anyone what I was going through. I'd made my choice and I had to stick with it.

I will tell you about one thing living on the campsite. Where it was situated there were a lot of horse stables. Charles was friends with one of the owners of the stable yard who said that we could ride the horses. We were having riding lessons and because I had my operation I was unable to continue but Charles and Murrey did. On this particular Sunday, it was a lovely autumn day, they had gone for their lessons and I was to follow on at my own pace. When I turned the corner to walk across the field to where they were having their riding lessons, I saw Charles flying through the air as the horse he was riding had thrown him off. Charles and the instructor took the horse back down to the yard and on seeing this Murrey's horse decided that he wasn't going to be left behind and the next thing you saw was Murrey hanging on to the horse for dear life onto, the instructor running hell for leather after him. I just couldn't do anything but watch in fear for Murrey. By some sheer miracle Murrey stopped the horse just before the fence with brambles on the other side of it. He got off the horse shaking and bless him, he got back on it.

Whilst I was walking along Sheerness High Street, I noticed an advert for a one night stay on the QE2 at a special price. I thought that would be a nice surprise to give to Charles as an early Christmas present. When I enquired about it, it was fully booked but I was placed onto the reserve list. It was on a Friday afternoon whilst we was taking Murrey to his father's for the weekend I received a call to say that we could go on the trip, obviously Charles was wondering what it was all about and I told him. He was absolutely over the moon. Then about a week later before we'd gone on the trip we had a disagreement about something and Charles turned to me viciously and said that he didn't want to go on the trip and not to bother with it. I'd already paid for it and he would have to lump it. Once again Charles wanted to destroy whatever pleasure I had. The trip for me was spoilt. Yes I can say I've been on the QE2 but it wasn't happy memories. He disappeared most of the time running around the ship like a little boy.

We saw 2000 in on the caravan site. Charles refused to go out to celebrate but he said I could if I wanted to knowing I couldn't go anywhere without him taking me. I will mention here that we'd moved into a very up market caravan, I must admit it was really lovely. We'd agreed that we would live on the site for the next five years to enable us to save up for a deposit on a house. I will add here again, it was Charles taking control once more. It was also on New Year's eve of 2000 when Amy rang me to tell me that she was engaged to be married, I was so happy for them.

Many things had happened so I'm going to skip it and go onto the next change. We moved again! For some crazy reason, Charles decided that we had to move. We bought a three storey house in Sheerness right opposite a Catholic church. It needed a lot of work doing to it. In the basement there was a living room, dining room, kitchen, shower and toilet, next floor up were two more rooms, an old kitchen and bathroom and on the third floor were two bedrooms. The house had been divided up into two flats at one time. You guessed it, not much work was done on this house either.

We were not the only residents living at this house. We had a spirit boy who used to sit on the stairs watching us in the dining room; I could never see him but Murrey and Charles could. He used to sit on the end of Murrey's bed and watch him, he was quite a playful soul. There were lots of other spirit energies in the house, so much so Charles asked a friend of ours if he would move them on to the higher realms. This he did by opening the portal in our living room so that those who would like to go home could leave through it.

Many left but there were a couple that stayed and they didn't cause a problems. There was one occasion when Charles was absolutely scared stiff. He was painting Murrey's bedroom and the bedroom door closed all by itself. There was nothing around that could have caused this to happen and Charles told me that he felt really uncomfortable, he felt that the spirit was sinister and just didn't know what to do. He would have jumped out of the bedroom window just to get away from it but he was three floors up!

I also have felt something really sinister. It wasn't in the house it was in Charles clinic. We used to take time out in giving each other treatments; massage for me and reflexology for Charles. It was on one occasion when I was giving Charles reflexology that I felt fear. I felt something really bad come into the room and for the first time in my life I was very frightened. I didn't let on to Charles what was going on but I nearly panicked and all of a sudden a thought came into my head to say the Lord's Prayer. When I finished saying it and asking for protection to surround me, the 'being' left.

Whilst we were living on the caravan site, we'd made friends with a couple and got talking about Spiritualism etc., and we decided that we would go into business together by opening a New Age shop offering different services, workshops etc. Because of his credit rating, the friend asked if I would take out a loan and put things in my name. You've got alarm bells ringing, and you would be right. It was the week before the shop was to open when he called me downstairs and said that he wanted me out and to take it over. Like a fool I agreed. It was horrible being there after my business partner said he wanted to take over. Why didn't I fight for the business? I think it was because Darren (business partner) was such a smooth talker in persuading me, after all he was a sales man in his last job. He said he would keep up the payments of the loan and take over everything else and I believed him. He did try to run the business with his wife and sister in-law. He even persuaded her to take a loan out presumably to pay me back but I never saw any of the money. Consequently after I'd opened a similar shop in Sheerness he sold the business in Chatham to someone else and kept the money, but I didn't realise the paperwork had not been completed. I was left to sort it out and to pay a lot of money to get out of the lease. Here was another man who had let me down. I thought I could trust him but he was no better than anyone else; he was so clever with words and playing with your mind too.

I know Charles wasn't really happy about my having my own business, but for once I dug my heels in and said that I was going for it. He did tell me that he wouldn't help me and I was to do it alone, although I did manage to get him to drive me to the suppliers every so often. The only reason he did so was I paid him for the petrol; I suppose that was fair. I employed a young man who would be working for me part time and it was he that helped me get the shop ready. I opened the Sheerness shop in September 2000.

CHAPTER 6

Opening day was a success and I really loved the work I was doing. What was even more enjoyable was meeting other likeminded spiritual people. There were many who asked what services I was providing such as readings, healing, running a circle etc. Thinking about it now, I feel that this shop was the foundation of what was to happen later on in my life. I learnt so much about Spiritualism. What I didn't know I found out and based on what I did know, I helped and advised others. I created such a calm atmosphere that people used to come into the shop, walk around it, then walk back out just to enjoy the experience. One person used to come in quite regularly and she told me why she didn't buy anything. Her visits were purely for the calming feelings she got from being in the shop. These helped her no end. I also found out that she was going through so much in her personal life and her visits to the shop helped her to cope.

I had many broken souls coming into that shop. They needed help and guidance. Some were being abused physically and sexually. All I could do was be there and listen. I could not intervene as it was not my job to do so. Only they could take the decision about the situation they were going through. I also performed some wonderful healing work and had some good results. One lady was going to have her womb taken away as she had cervical cancer. She was only in her twenties. She was a Reiki Master and I said, 'why don't we work on the healing together?' She was due to have her operation a couple of weeks later so we got down to it. I saw a lot of 'muck' and between us we got rid of it with the healing power of Spirit. She went to the hospital for a pre-op check and when the consultant looked at her womb she was shocked as there was absolutely nothing wrong with it. Everything was looking very healthy and needless to say she didn't have the operation.

There were two more healing wonders that Spirit performed. The first one was to help a young lady who was told she would never be able to conceive and after working with reflexology combined with healing she became pregnant and had a baby boy. The second concerned someone who had cancerous cells in her lungs. After receiving healing over a period of time she went back to her consultants and had the tests to see how her condition had progressed and the tests found nothing amiss. The doctors just couldn't understand it. On this particular healing, I laid my hands on the affected area around the front near her shoulder and she used to say can I take my hand back a bit as she said she could feel that something or someone was seemingly operating on her and she could feel the pain or heat. There were times when my healing energies used to change from hot to freezing cold, this was a new experience for me as I always thought it had to be hot, not so. My guides told me that it all depends on the condition that they are working on, on what energies that is right at the time. One thing I used to notice was whenever I asked for my healing guides to work with me I always felt that I had to stand with my legs quite apart with knees bent as I felt my guide that was stepping in was a shorter person than myself and my hands seem to feel larger. I don't know who my guides are, with the exception of one and he's a very special man to me and has always come to me in times of distress. He is like a big cuddly bear and I'm sure he's grinning as I'm saying this. He appears to me wearing two different colour robes depending on what situation is going on with me; it can be either a silver white or a beautiful royal blue, a staff in his hand that looks to be of twisted wood with amethyst stone on the top of the staff, a chain with a big amethyst stone in the middle. He has long grey/white beard and long hair and has these most amazing blue eyes which I can't describe, that draws you to him. He says his name is Moses.

I find when I'm working with Spirit giving evidence that the client or a member of the audience seems to be so concerned with who their guides are. You tend to find it's always an Indian, a Nun, wise Chinaman etc., it may not be any of these. It can be a chimney sweep boy, a parlour maid of old, a monk, an angel or indeed even your own relative. I feel that I don't need to know who my guides are as they swop and change according to the circumstances I'm going through. I do feel that if you keep worrying about who your guides are, you are not allowing the flow of the communication, take it from me, I've been there. It got to the point when I said 'okay, that's it, just get on with it and if you really need me to know then I will listen'.

I couldn't understand about the power of healing as I've never been shown or taught, it was something I was instinctively drawn to. I was drawn to just lay my hands on a person and just let Spirit step in and take over. I never questioned what my healing guides were doing. I do have a lovely memory of giving healing to a brother and sister. We were in the back room of the shop and my client was laying down on the healing couch. I was giving healing to the brother and the sister was watching me. When I'd finished she said she could see all this white light energy surrounding my hands and I thought I wasn't channelling anything, there has been many occasions that has happened and the client may say they felt a lot of things happening, even they have felt someone else around them, there can be anything from one to about four spirits helping in the healing process. You may ask at times when you see people suffering with cancer, depression and other illnesses, why the person can't be fully healed. I've asked that question many times and this is the answer I've been given by my guides. You all have a lesson or a journey that needs to be completed. That is why you are here. You may be working through a karma from a past life for you to experience the pain or emotions. If your guides didn't think you could do it or you are not strong enough to do it, they wouldn't put you through it. I just trusted them. However, I must tell you that once I left my shop a couple of years later, I didn't do any more healing for many years.

During the time at the shop I heard so many sad stories that all I could do was listen as there was nothing I could do. Young ladies who were being sexually abused by prominent people in society that you would never dream would do what they were doing to their own children, women with abusive husbands, people who were suicidal, some who were depressed; they all came to my shop. I was glad that

I was there to be able to listen to these affected souls as they had no one else to turn to. There were some who were micky takers and I spotted them. There were also some who just wanted to come in and try and get a free reading, or get a reading if they were under the age of eighteen as I didn't agree to giving readings to children. Firstly, I would need their parents' permission and secondly they've not had enough life experiences. My spirit guides, told me to be wary and I heeded their advice. I had spiritual people come into the shop when I needed help with certain problems or situations' somehow spirit provided me with the answers I needed. I learnt about moving 'stuck spirits', these are entities that have not gone to the light to cross over, which helped me so much for the work I was to do later on. I believe that the people you meet on your life's journey are there for a reason, this could be to help, guide, challenge, show you the way or give you guidance.

I began to talk in 'spirit tongue' more and more when I felt that I had to ask for the 'higher beings' help. I just knew when I started speaking that the energy changed and things were going to be okay. You may be asking 'what is this spirit tongue she keeps going on about?' I will try and explain it as best as I can. If you remember, I said that when I became a born again Christian I started speaking in spirit tongue. This is when you start getting strange words coming continuously in your head. You close your eyes and just let the energy flow and the words just come out. Its sounds all gobbledy-gook and strangely foreign but when I start to speak this language a huge wave of spiritual energy overcomes me. You just have to trust in what you are saying as somehow spirit seems to understand and things start to sort themselves out. There have been many a times when I've used spirit tongue when I've been so frustrated and angry; it's a way of venting off your frustration and enabling you to get on with your life. I suppose one way to look at it is that your earthly soul still remembers being a spirit in the wonderful world you have left to be here on the Earth plane to undertake the work you have chosen and because in the spirit world life is so much simpler, you can't cope with the difficulties you encounter every day. Having the joy of using spirit tongue enables you to feel that connection with the spirit world.

When I opened the shop I mentioned that I employed a part timer, whose name was Adam. He was a great help to me in the shop and I used to leave the shop in his hands on Wednesdays which enabled me to have a day off or go and buy more stock. I then began to hear stories of what he was doing behind my back. He used to give healing in the back room and we had a donations box there for freewill offerings. What he used to do was place a twenty pound note in the box because people used to wonder how much to put in it so they copied and then he'd take the money out and put it in his pocket. He did this several times. He gave readings and he was supposed to be very good as he had been recommended to me by others. I had to give a refund on one occasion as the client felt very uncomfortable; she felt he was making sexual advances to her. He was also becoming weird with regards to the 'aliens' that were coming to him during his meditation. I now know that aliens can come to you as I have a better understanding of the different worlds, at that time I just thought he was off the wall. He would even go up to people in the street and give them off the cuff messages which frightened them. One person was heavily pregnant and he was giving her doom and gloom about the baby, even suggesting that the baby wasn't going to make it and another was to my friend when he turned round and implied that her mother had died that day, after which she went into a panic trying to get hold of her mother, whom I'm happy to say had not died. The last straw was when I found out that Adam was entertaining ladies in my absence and that they were aware of my takings and what was going on in the business. I just had to let him go. I heard he became a Jehovah Witness condemning Spiritualists and Spiritualism, saying we are of the devil and are evil. Talk about going from one extreme to another. Now we are all condemned to hell!

I was still attending my local spiritualist church as I found it a haven to get away from Charles. I used to receive a lot of messages from loved ones and was constantly being told that I would be doing the same as the Medium, giving off messages, and I said 'no way'. Never say 'no way' where spirit are concerned as they will find a way of getting you there. They really are very crafty! The President of Sheerness Spiritualist Church came up to me one day after I received a message about going on the rostrum, and asked me if I would give it a go. Before I could even think about it, my mouth said these strange words – yes, (gulp)! When you are booked to do a Divine Service you have to know how to open in prayer, give an address in whatever you are inspired to talk about, and do the demonstration of mediumship whereby you are connecting the two worlds together to give messages. It's a bit like having a telephone conversation when at times the phone connection is a bit dodgy and you may get the message slightly wrong, it's very hard work and requires a huge amount of trust.

The day arrived when I took the Divine Service and I was really nervous. I've been told that this is good being nervous. Firstly its spirits way of saying they are with you and secondly, the day you don't feel these nerves is the day you pack it in as the energy is so different. There are stories I've heard that Mediums tend to have alcohol before working to give them courage and this is a very, very big no-no. This affects the way you work and can lead you to become dependent on drink. There have been times when I've wanted wine with my lunch and I get this 'don't you dare!' in my ear so I obeyed. Shame, really. They taught me a lesson on this. I'd had several glasses before doing a party reading and I just couldn't get anything, the link was gone and I gave myself the bad name of being a rubbish Medium. Lesson learnt.

Before Charles and I went to the church, he turned to me and said 'I don't want you coming to me to give me a message' and I said, 'Don't worry, I've already got a message for you,' and told him what spirit were giving me. It was something he'd done that week and I knew nothing about it. His mother was saying thank you for the carnations he'd put on their grave, (his father was in the same burial plot). It was proof to me spirit and I were connected. I even remembered what I was wearing – a red suit with a white blouse. The evening went really well. The only bit I didn't like doing was the address and I'm afraid I'm still like that today. Cheryl was there too as she was a long serving member of the church and she told me afterwards she was panicking for me and keeping her eyes closed all through the service, bless her.

The business in Sheerness expanded with more and more stock being added. I was selling crystals, metaphysical ornaments, incense sticks, jewellery and lots of other new age stuff. I just ploughed all the money I had into it and didn't take anything out for myself. It was a big shop to fill but, unfortunately, I feel the New Age boom was beginning to decline and I wasn't aware of this happening until I closed the shop and noticed how few 'New Age' shops there still were.

My relationship with Charles really wasn't all that fantastic by this time. We just got on with things. He was still trying to control many aspects of Murrey's life and mine. We continued to do things behind his back. He didn't like my children and family or friends coming to the house and made it uncomfortable for them. One petty thing he did was to refuse to give them sugar in their hot drink or allow anyone to eat crisps or apples, anything that made a noise. It was fine for his friends and family to visit and Charles made them very welcome. Let's just say, I got my justice many years later. Karma has a way of paying debts. Don't ever think if you do something really wrong against someone, you will get away with it because you won't. There has to be a balance, a yin and yang.

It was in this shop that I met my very best friend Maria. She came in one day and seemed very troubled. I soon realised that she didn't have much money either so I offered to give her a mini reading free of charge. This reading proved to be life changing for her and stopped her going down a particular road. Maria is an Angel in disguise. We have helped each other in so many ways over the years and have always been there for each other. I have rescued her from many situations and there were a few; I know she doesn't mind me saying this. She was there for me when I was going through the most frightening time of my life which I will tell you about later, and I love her for it.

It was now 2001. Mum and I went on a mother's day trip to Jersey; a place where she had always wanted to go. The trip was my gift to her and I know Charles wasn't happy about my going. Mum and I really had a lovely time and spent some real quality time together. Mum hadn't been feeling well for a long time; she was suffering from a hiatus hernia and she also had some ulcers which had burst a couple of times. This made Mum very ill as all the poison was going into her body.

Also in that year, Amy gave birth to her second son Tyler. He was born in May and it was a good pregnancy and he held on to full term. As you can imagine Amy did worry in case he arrived early like his brother.

It was in July of 2001 when I went over to visit Mum in Gravesend. We'd gone into town for lunch and walked back to her house. We'd stopped at the riverside park in Gravesend and were talking about different things, about my relationship with Charles and about the new baby. Amy had come over earlier that day and spent time with her nan. It was whilst we were sitting there mum turned to me and said that she loved me very much. I was really touched by this as she had never told me she loved me before. This was the last time I was to speak to her.

One night a few days later, in the early hours of the morning we received a phone call to get to Darenth Valley Hospital near Dartford, as Mum had been rushed there and immediately taken down to theatre. As you can imagine I was in a turmoil and just wanted to get to the hospital to be with her. Prior to this, Charles' car had been playing up and I kept telling him to get it sorted. Needless to say it was on this night the car broke down on the other side of Medway tunnel. We were unaware that there had been an attempt to hold up the petrol station in Frindsbury Road and the police were everywhere. Luckily for me, one very kind policeman asked us what was wrong and when we explained and he gave us a lift to Darenth Valley Hospital in the back of the police car. So we arrived courtesy of the boys in blue! I was being looked after that night by the angels; they knew I had to get to the hospital to be with Mum.

The rest of the family were there and the surgeon came up to explain what was wrong with Mum. He asked us if she was to die on the operating table, should he attempt resuscitation. We all agreed that Mum wouldn't want to be brought back and that we should let her go. What had happened was that an ulcer had burst and it was a bad one. They said they would do all they could for her. Charles wouldn't stay with me; he wanted to get back to his car and get home so he left. I was so angry. The one time I really needed him and he wasn't there.

Mum came out of theatre and was taken into the Intensive Care Unit. She never regained consciousness as the infection was too bad. Charles kept making my life difficult when I wanted to go and see her. I had to make the journey by train. It was on a Thursday when I received a call from Amy telling me to get to the hospital; again Charles wouldn't help. I went by train so far and Amy picked me up and took me to the hospital. When we arrived we were told that Mum didn't have long to live. We all gathered around her bed. I was watching the monitor all the time and it was almost at the end I knew she was struggling.

I bent over her ear and said, "It's okay, Mum, you can go." The minute I said that, she died

After a while, I went out and phoned Charles I was very upset with tears rolling down my face. Charles' reaction was to tell me to pull myself together and get on with it. I swore at him and put the phone down on him.

Whilst lying in bed that evening after Mum had passed, I was thinking about Mum and I distinctly felt someone come to the side of the bed and give me a kiss on the cheek. I just knew it was her saying she was alright. It was a few months later when I was asleep, I was in that in-between kind of sleep when Mum came to me. She looked so radiant and I said, "Mum, you're alive!"

She smiled at me and then faded. I knew then that there was definitely a spirit world.

The day of the funeral arrived. Sadly, Martin's mother passed away the day before so the poor children lost both their grandmothers within a couple of weeks of each other. My family just didn't want Charles in the main car with us and nor did I but he just pushed his way in and said he was coming. We had the last laugh, when he stepped into the car his trousers ripped from the front to the back. I could imagine Mum laughing her head off; I know we did. Charles kept telling me that I mustn't cry, keep a stiff upper lip, I cried all through the service and when Mum was being lowered into the ground. The first person I turned to was Martin and my children. Charles never forgave me for doing this as he felt I should have turned to him. I was past caring.

Unfortunately I didn't grieve till about 2008 and it was whilst writing the first draft of my book that I was able to really cry; to let go. There is never a right time to stop grieving. Many people would say pull yourself together, its time you got over it. It takes as long as it takes so don't ever feel guilty. There is never a wrong or a right way. It's what you are going through and how you deal with it should be a matter for you.

Charles became involved in a charity helping people in Sarajevo which was very commendable of him. Again he was really doing it for his own selfish reasons. I know this sounds harsh but he was desperate to earn a medal somewhere and had even approached the Bosnian army to enlist, without asking me or telling me of his intentions. As you can guess they turned him down. Goes to show that he wasn't thinking of me doesn't it? He went out to Bosnia to help the victims of the war by giving them massage treatments and I'm sure he helped them no end. That's one thing I can say about Charles. He was extremely good at his job and knew what he was doing. He could always get to the root cause of the problem and solve it. He went out to Sarajevo twice and it was on the second visit he left me for six weeks with only one hundred pounds for food. I did struggle and at the same time was so angry. The anger was because he couldn't afford to leave his own business for that length of time as all the time he was in Sarajevo he was not earning any money. He had to pay for all of his expenses for food and flight etc.

I don't know the full story of what happened in Sarajevo, but Charles was not asked to work for the charity again. I never did find out what he got up to out there.

Charles was very involved with the Freemasons. He used to leave me a couple of times in the week of the evening to attend these meetings, not just in his own lodge; he travelled to other lodges. I became interested in Freemasonry and wondered what it was all about. I'd heard they raised a lot of money for good causes and they used to have wonderful meals after their meetings. Sounds good to me.

One day, after Charles had been to a meeting, I asked him more questions about what they get up to and he said that there was a very strong lady masons group on the Island. If I would like to join, he would put out feelers for me. The day arrived when I was called for an interview by the lady masons. When I arrived, there was a group of ladies sitting there and I was introduced to them. I must admit, it's a bit nerve wracking sitting there in front of all these 'important' ladies. You could sense that they were not short of a few bob and had lovely homes, whereas I was skint and didn't have a nice home. The interview went well, and they would confirm to me later once I've had my police check whether I've been successful or not.

I can't remember how I got the news but I was accepted. I had a lady who was to be my sponsor and mentor, she would help me through my very first meeting. Obviously I didn't know what to expect as you hear so many stories about freemasonry but it wasn't bad at all. The lady masons have now been going for over a hundred years and they are a very strong movement. They do exactly the same as the men, only better, apparently.

In Freemasonry you work your way up the ranks, becoming officers and then finally the Master. I got to Junior Warden when I had to give it up. I did enjoy the banquets and the dressing up in our finest clothes but I felt that the ladies were rather cliquey and it's a case of if your face fits then you were okay.

There were some lovely ladies whom I got on well with but I always felt I had to be careful in what I said, the reason being they all knew Charles very well as he had grown up with a lot of them and I didn't want to let out of the bag what my plans were. I did hear that he wasn't as popular in the Craft as he thought he was as they didn't like how he conducted his affairs.

On the day Murrey left school, he left home and went to live with his father. I couldn't blame him for that but I really missed him and I felt so alone.

I was becoming more and more unhappy and realised that I was more often unhappy than happy. I had to do something about this so I decided to close the shop when the lease expired in September of 2004. I sold as much stock as I could and I got a friend to take what was left over. All through the year I kept being told that I was going to Canada; drastic I know. Little did I realise this was a focus, an aim. Spirit wasn't daft; they knew me better. It was a sad day when I closed the shop for the last time and I felt I had learnt so much. I also hope that I helped many.

Also in September of 2004 Amy got married. I'd gone to her house the night before to be with her when she woke up in the morning. The day was absolutely beautiful weather wise and Amy looked beautiful too. My brother and I arrived at the car park and walked across it to get to the register office at The Bishops Palace in Maidstone and I saw this man wearing a funny hat little realising that it was Charles wearing a pith helmet!

I was so angry when I saw him and said, "Why are you wearing that stupid hat?"

His reply was, "Because I've got a headache!"

I just said normal people take headache tablets. I'd also noticed that he was wearing the scruffiest of his suits as he had some really smart suits, he just went out of his way to embarrass me. It back fired because he was a laughing stock and I just kept my distance from him the rest of the day. I'm also happy to say he wasn't in any of the official wedding pictures.

We went to a hotel for the reception and I was sitting at the top main table. It came to the speeches and we started to toast those who were not with us such as the two grandparents. Just as the best man mentioned my mum's name a balloon popped right next to me. There was no one standing anywhere near it; it was like she was saying 'I'm here!'

What I've noticed here is that Charles wanted to be the centre of attention. He wanted to destroy any happiness I was having with my family or indeed in any other situation. He just liked to control me and that didn't last much longer.

My daughter Amy and the rest of the family knew what I was going to do and they were all for it. What they thought about me going to Canada I don't know. I was nuts! Thinking about it now, I think I was heading for a break down and wasn't thinking rationally. All I wanted to do was get away from Charles.

The trouble with Charles was that he had two sides. He could be so charming, fun, amusing, and generous at times, so you think you've made a mistake and try and make a go of the marriage then the dark side comes out. It was a constant mind game; mental cruelty some would say.

I left Charles in October 2004 and went to Amy's house. He thought I had gone away with friends on holiday. The thing is, he knew I wasn't going with friends and he didn't stop me. I flew out to Nova Scotia in Canada on 1st November 2004.

CHAPTER 7

I arrived in Halifax, Nova Scotia early in the evening and went out to find a taxi to take me to my final destination some two hundred and fifty miles away. The taxi driver was a really nice guy but the journey took hours.

I was viewing a property that had been divided into many apartments and I was looking to see if I could buy the business. What the hell was I thinking off? The lady who was looking after the property let me in and I had a choice of any room I wanted. I was really tired so I chose the first room she showed me so that I could get myself into bed as soon as possible.

I was sorting out my clothes when a voice told me to go back home! What? I said, you want me to go home? And the resounding answer back was yes. I slept that night and the next morning I went out exploring. The area was very nice but remote and it would have been so difficult for me to live there as I would definitely have needed to drive and I can't. So I phoned for a taxi and retraced the two hundred and fifty miles back to Halifax. The lady taxi driver took me to a bed and breakfast place which was stunning and the people running it were lovely. The next day I went to the airport to buy my return flight ticket back home. Whilst there I asked a taxi driver to take me around the city of Halifax as I thought I might as well see something of the place. It's a beautiful place to visit.

Thinking about what I did, I was crazy! How the hell was I going to even be able to buy such a property and run it on my own? I knew no one and had a sight problem. It shows you how desperate I was to get away. I feel, looking back at it now, that it was spirit's way of getting me away and helping me to realise that I could do anything I wanted. I have the strength inside of me to do this! The flight back was a little bumpy when we were coming into land at St Johns airport, so much so I grabbed the leg of the guy that was sitting next to me. I bet he thought he was being attacked! I was full of apologies and we both laughed about it.

I arrived back at Heathrow airport and there was loads of messages on my mobile from Charles wanting to know where I was. I forgot to mention that Charles had decided that he was going to sell our house and move onto a much smaller property which again needed a lot of work doing to it. That was the straw that broke the camel's back. He was concerned because there were papers to sign and he needed my signature. I told him I was at Heathrow airport and was on my way back home to Amy. Charles had also received my letter telling him that I had left him and that I would not be coming back. I know it was a coward's way of doing it but it was the only way I could cope.

Amy came and collected me and took me to her home. It was a few days later from arriving home that I realised I had to look for somewhere to live, sleeping on an airbed was very uncomfortable. We started by looking through newspapers and after a couple of days we spotted a two bedroomed house within my budget for rent. Amy phoned the contacts number and whilst she was talking to the lady on the phone I had a vision of the property and I couldn't believe what I was seeing. I went to view the property and it turned out to be the very house I had seen in my vision. I just couldn't believe it. When I married Martin in 1976 we moved into the forth house down on the left hand side in Nash Close. The house I now moved into was exactly the same but in the opposite road to Nash Close; forth house up and on the left hand side. This house was my saviour.

What was even more amazing was that the house had already been rented out and the people who were just about to move in had managed to get themselves a council property. The timing was perfect and I had just enough money to pay the deposit and first month's rent.

You approached this house by walking up the front garden where there was a carport. The front door led into a hall and turned left where there were stairs and you went through a door into the living room, then into the kitchen/diner. Upstairs at the head of the stairs was the bathroom and then two bedrooms. The house was basically furnished but was comfortable. Amazingly it had the exact same boiler and bathroom suite as my old house in Nash Close. The garden was really lovely and peaceful. I called this house my healing house. It really allowed me the time to sort my life out.

I moved in on 15th November 2004 with just my two suitcases. Amy and I went out and bought the bedding, towels, china, kettle etc. I felt very at home. I did struggle for a while financially until I could get my money sorted. There were times when I couldn't afford to have the heating on and I used to lay on the settee with the quilt over me and a hat on my head. Amy came round a couple of times and brought me some food such as bread, eggs, potatoes etc. Gradually things did improve for me.

Charles was being an absolute nuisance; he just wouldn't leave me alone and wouldn't heed my requests not to call me. I even cried begging him to leave me alone, and as usual, what Charles wanted Charles thought he could get. There was a time when I was beginning to waver, and Amy told me if ever I thought about going back to him she would lock me in the cupboards until I came to my senses. Needless to say, I didn't go back to Charles!

Eventually I plucked up enough courage to speak to Charles and tell him there was no going back. Before I did speak to Charles, I asked for the angels to help me find the words and not to change my mind. Boy! Did I let him have it! I felt very strong and as I looked into his eyes and I think he knew that I wasn't going to change my mind.

Talking about the angels, whenever I needed help with money to buy food, or money to buy a freezer the angels helped me; they helped me to somehow find the money. There was one occasion when I made a list of what I needed, it was clothes for the winter, a mobile phone because mine was breaking down, a computer and a couple of other bits. I just left it with the angels. A few days later, Jennifer rang me and said would I like one thousand pounds, no strings attached? She didn't want the money back and as you can imagine I said yes and went out and bought everything that was on the list. Jennifer had just got her divorce settlement and she just wanted shot of it. I will always be grateful to Jennifer, she came into my life to help me get onto the spiritual pathway and help me with getting me on my feet. I owe her a lot.

I was settling in nicely and getting on with my life. I'd spent a lot of time thinking, trying to work out the direction I was going. Mind you, it's very difficult to make plans if you have a disability and live on benefits as the system doesn't make it easy for you to try and get out the trap you're in.

My friend Maria was going through some pretty hard times too. She used to come and stay with me and we really had some good times going out for walks, watching films and chilling out. She loved coming to the house too as she felt she could completely unwind. By this time we had a special friendship where I would help her in her hour of need and she would help me in turn.

It was 2005 and Charles was still playing with my emotions. He'd turn up with holiday brochures about all the trips that I wanted to go on. He'd tell me he would take me out to wonderful places. I just couldn't take any more of it. I was asleep one night having previously been crying my eyes out asking God to not let me wake up in the morning when, at about two in the morning, I saw this being. I couldn't tell you if it was a male or female; it was like a grey white energy and I didn't feel frightened. In its hand was a golden ball of energy and the being placed this golden ball of energy in the small of my back. The sensation of this was so much so that I cried out 'ooh'. I felt that sensation for days afterwards and the memory has stayed with me. It was after this that my life began to change for the better.

As a result of the actions of Darren, my previous business partner, I was heavily in debt. The only way out of the situation was to declare myself bankrupt. Charles paid the court fees and he said that no matter what he would support me.

I was made bankrupt for a year, but it's not a nice thing to have to go through. When you become bankrupt, it doesn't matter how healthy your own personal bank account is. You can be in credit and never have overdrawn your account; the bank immediately closes that account along with any other accounts you may hold. If you have a savings account with another bank then that is immediately closed too. The only way you can have an account is by trying to find a bank that will allow you to open an account but you will only have a cash card account. The banking institutions are so insensitive. The whole situation may not have been your fault, and they make you feel like a criminal and degrade you as there is not a shred of sympathy. You are a nothing.

Even though you are declared bankrupt for a year, it's on your records for seven years. You cannot get anywhere. After you have gone through the year you then have to obtain your Discharge from Bankruptcy certificate which costs you even more money. They get you every which way they can.

What finally told Charles it was over was my having a liaison with a much older man; there were twenty-two years between us. I'd known him for a while, he came to my wedding when I married Charles. I'd bumped into him in Chatham and we immediately struck up a friendship. He was such a charming man and he asked if I would like to go to Spain with him to stay with some friends he knew out there. I told him that I didn't have any money to pay for the flight but he said he would pay for me. It was a lovely holiday out there, just what I needed. He was such a gentleman but I began to notice he was beginning to control me and my life. The relationship lasted for a year before I told him it was over. He started to behave just like Charles, didn't like me having my friends and family around and he seem to ask questions about my every move. He used to play with my mind by saying just enough to make me doubt myself by saying his guides were telling him what I was up to and that scared me. It made me feel that I was being watched at all times. He would go out to buy a newspaper and he'd sit on a bench and that was when 'Spirit' was supposed to tell him about me. Actually he would creep back into the house if I was on the phone talking to a friend of mine and stand in the upstairs back bedroom listening to everything I was saying. He frightened the life out of me when I discovered what he'd done. It wasn't long after that situation when he was coming down the stairs when I suddenly heard the sound of a fall. He was lying on the floor with a cut to his head. I called my brother in-law and we got him to hospital to have his wound looked at. He told me that he felt he was pushed down the stairs. He distinctly felt something like a hand on his back.

I know now I had a guide standing at the head of the stairs. I was being protected at all times but I didn't think he would do such a thing as push him. My two grandsons had seen my guide as they told me they didn't like to go upstairs to the bathroom because a man was standing there.

I did learn one thing from this liaison; that was to recognise what was going on around me and to be strong enough to do something about it and not to go back. This man taught me about woodcarving which I really enjoyed doing. They say having such an age gap doesn't matter, yes it does! You become the child in the relationship even though you are meant to be on equal terms.

Talking about spirits in my saviour house, there was a lot of activity. I swear the old man that died in the bedroom I slept in used to visit often. I would feel someone getting into bed beside me and when I became aware of it I used to tell him to hop it! On another occasion I went away to the Arthur Findlay College at Stanstead in Essex for a week and Maria was going through rough times. So I arranged with her to stay at my place for a couple of days and to sleep in my bed. On the first night she was there, she'd settled down to sleep and it was in the early hours of the morning she felt herself pushed to one side of the bed so that her nose nearly touched the bedside cabinet. She woke up and swore at the spirit entity and told it to leave. Needless to say, she kept the light on all night!

Maria and I were watching a video on another occasion and all of a sudden the dragonfly ornament on top of the television went flying across the room. I told the spirit to pack it in. On still another occasion, Maria again came to stay and I was sleeping on the airbed in the living room and I was just dozing when I heard the door open and someone walking across the airbed to get to the kitchen and back again. I asked Maria if she had come down during the night and she said no However, I never ever felt frightened living in that house. It was my haven. It allowed me to sort my emotions out and to begin to heal myself.

In 2006 I had some wonderful news from Amy that she was expecting another baby and was so hoping that it was going to be a girl. Also in that year, Amy said wasn't it about time that I applied for another guide dog. Again I was hesitant and as usual Amy talked me round. I contacted Guide Dogs again; I wasn't sure I would be accepted bearing in mind that I had given Samba up before. But I'm happy to say they said yes and sent someone out from Guide Dogs to see me and re-access me. Again I was very lucky because I didn't have to wait too long before they had the right dog for me. This is when Willow entered my life.

Willow was an eighteen-month old golden retriever. He had just finished his training and was now looking for his first owner and it happened to be me. We hit it off straight away. My training with Willow was going to start in the New Year of 2007. I was going to be picked up each day by taxi to be taken to a hotel in Maidstone from where I would go out with Willow. Willow would also be staying with me each night too so that we could bond and get to know each other. There were some fraught times during the training, so much so that I said I didn't want to have Willow or any other guide dog for that matter. As usual it was Amy who sorted me out. Willow was always very strong willed and I'm the same. That's why guide dogs paired us up together.

It was February 2007 when I received a phone call from Amy to say that she had given birth to a baby girl. They called her Louise, and this is Amy's middle name. After I took the call, I burst out crying and Willow came up to me and pushed his head against my leg to ask if I was okay.

Even after I'd qualified with Willow, he still tested me and again Amy had to persuade me not to send him back. He had walked me down the middle of the road towards oncoming traffic, he had taken me down paths that I didn't want to go down and wouldn't obey certain commands. I was so thankful that I had some vision otherwise it would have been very frightening indeed if I'd been totally blind.

Willow was such a character. He was gentle, trusting, and cheeky and he was mine. I'm so glad that I kept him. He was a very special dog, he was a healing dog; he gave healing and unconditional love to all those he met and I have had some wonderful times with him. He was great in getting me safely home after I'd had a couple of glasses of wine with a friend of mine over lunch, I'd just say to him 'take me home' and he did.

In April of 2008, I received a phone call telling me that the owner of the saviour house had passed away the night before and I was being given a week's notice to leave the property. As you can imagine I went into panic mode again wondering how I was going to find somewhere to live in a week. Luckily for me, spirit gave me a message and I followed up on what they said.

I went firstly to the council to see if they could help me and they said no. Even with a disability you do not get any help. I then went to Shelter and they were very very helpful and told me of my legal rights. I had to be served with an eviction notice of two months; the landlady just couldn't tell me to get out. I gave a sigh of relief and told my landlady the legal procedures and she then sorted it out. Mind you, she did become a pest as she was phoning me nearly every day asking how the search for alternative accommodation was going.

Amy and I started looking and phoning around for properties to rent. It was even more difficult as I had to find a one bedroomed property and one that would allow me to take Willow. You wouldn't believe the difficulties in trying to find a place to live. Eventually I spotted one in the paper and something was saying don't touch that one. Amy had seen it as well and asked me whether I had phoned about it; I nearly lied and said that it had already gone. In some ways I wished it had gone. We went to view it, and as time was running out I accepted it. I moved in in May 2008.

CHAPTER 8

This time I moved back to Twydall. I was only 150 yards away from where I previously lived with Martin in Preston Way. One thing I've noticed is that my life goes round in circles. It seems that I have lessons to learn or maybe certain people to help.

The flat I moved into was a ground floor apartment with a utility room, one bedroom, bathroom, living room and a very big kitchen/diner. The flat was part of a chalet type house and the landlords used to come and stay in the rooms upstairs at weekends, (they lived in London). All I can say about them is that they turned out to be not as nice as you thought they were on first acquaintance. At the back of the flat was a very tiny garden surrounded by bamboo fencing. This was a tiny bit of ground when you looked at the size of the rest of the garden. There was a feeling of being hemmed in. The only trouble with the flat was the stairs attached at the back of the house that led upstairs. I didn't feel I had any privacy as I felt that the landlords kept looking through the window to see what was going on and they could listen to your conversation.

I'd got settled in and then decided to go out and explore my surroundings. I decided to take Willow to a field and to get to this field I had to catch a bus. When I got to the bus stop, there was a lady waiting and I asked her what time the next bus was due and don't ask me why but I told her I'd just moved into the area and that I was a Spiritualist Medium, doh! For some reason this was something she needed to know. She sat next to me on the bus and asked me what my guide dog's name was and I said Willow. This excited her even more, we found out we lived quite close to each other and I gave her my mobile number so she could explain why it meant so much to her.

I found out her name, it was Tracey. Tracey came round later that afternoon with a picture of her dog named Willow and she believes in coincidences and that they are meant for a reason. As it turned out, she'd just been going through a horrendous time with her ex-partner committing suicide and she was trying to cope with everything that was going on around her. My meeting her was a step towards helping her. I also needed some guidance and was looking for a Medium for a reading. Tracey gave me this guy's number and I rang him; managed to get an appointment that very evening. What was even more amazing was that I'd met Nigel many years ago when I'd had a reading from him. Nigel was to play an important part in my life and in my development of Spiritualism.

Nigel and I struck up a great friendship and he is one of my closest friends today. He helped me to understand about the way I was working from the rostrum in Spiritualist churches as I felt I wasn't any good. I used to compare myself with other Mediums and kept thinking that what I was doing was wrong. Nigel told me there was no right or wrong way of working for spirit. We are all unique in our own way which is the way our guides wish to work with us. It was one of the most important lessons I learnt. I also began to develop my interest in Spiritualism more and more. It's as if spirit were saying, you are now ready, you've just got a couple of things to sort out and you will be well and truly on the right path.

The first thing I had to sort out was my divorce from Charles. I'd made my final decision to move on from Charles on New Year's Day of 2008 and I wrote him a letter telling him that I would be filing for a divorce. If he contested the divorce, I would put everything in the petition about what he had done to me over the years. Needless to say he agreed as he didn't want all that coming out to sully his name. We were divorced in September 2008. The relief I felt was enormous but painful at the same time. It was another failed marriage and I really didn't want this to happen again. I was told nearly all relationships have their cut off point whereby you cannot keep working at something when the other person is not 'in' the relationship. It's a painful thing to recognise; to know when to walk away. People hang on for fear of the unknown but why be unhappy most of your life when you can be happy and acknowledge who you truly are. Life is so short, live it!

The other thing I had to sort out was my original book. I'd already got up as far as my mother's passing. I just couldn't get past that point. I was now ready to put the words down on paper and to finally grieve for my darling Mum.

Once I'd done that, oh boy, what a change to my life was yet to come, for once I can say a happy change.

Firstly, I must tell you about my fantastic bed. Bed? I hear you ask. I'd decided to decorate my bedroom and to make it mine. I'd already had some of my furniture delivered from Charles house that I'd paid for. My friend Tracey said she had a cast iron and brass bed she wanted to sell and I said yes please. This bed was over one hundred years old and it's the most comfortable bed I've ever slept on. I bought a wonderful rocking chair from Tracey as well.

Tracey had told me what had happened to her in that bed and they were not happy memories. I also felt there was a lot of energies attached to the bed and some of them were rather unsavoury. I then performed a clearance of negative energies and replaced them with pure white light and love. The energy in the bedroom changed dramatically. What a lot of people are not aware of is that good or bad energies can attach to anything and when things begin to go wrong people can't understand why these negative events should be happening. If you feel that you are going through such negativity, think back to when it all started. Was it when you bought something second-hand? Was it when you were given something? It could be absolutely anything, or that you moved into a property that had a lot of history. This could be the starting point. Once you recognise what it is, you may need to get some advice or find someone who is a Medium (best place to find a Medium is from a Spiritualist church) and get them to move on or cleanse the energies. It's as simple as that!

There is one energy I really do miss. One night I felt something four legged jump up onto the bed, walk upwards and make itself comfortable on the pillow at the top of the bed. I'd 'hear' a cat purring and also feel his claws going in and out. It used to come and visit me a lot and now he seems to have moved on. I do miss him. I told Tracey about this cat and she was amazed as she said that the 'cat' used to do it to her. I guess the spirit cat loved that bed. I used to have a lot of spiritual happenings in that flat.

One night, I'd only been asleep for about an hour when I heard padding of footsteps of a dog and a tail wagging which was banging on the side of the bed.

I turned over and spoke and said, "Willow, lay down!"

When I reached out my hand to pat Willow's head, there was nothing there which caused me to put my lamp on and I looked at the bedroom door to see if it was open, it was shut. The spirit dog I feel was my old guide dog Samba coming to say hello but I sent him away and he hasn't been back to me since.

I'm now going to go back a little in time. You remember I mentioned about Richard who used to run a development circle? Our paths kept crossing over the years and there was one time when Richard nearly kissed me in the shop I used to have in Sheerness, thankfully nothing happened. He was in a relationship and I heard that he got married to Melissa. When I heard this I was really disappointed, don't ask me why I should have been. When we nearly had that close encounter, I rang Richard and he was rather short with me to the point of being rude, so I didn't like him from then on.

Back to 2008; I'd heard on the grapevine that Richard's wife, Melissa, had passed away from a brain tumour in August. Then in late September I kept getting this voice in my head telling me to ring him. I couldn't imagine why I should, so I said to spirit no. This went on for a couple of weeks and finally I relented. It was eight thirty in the morning. I still had Richard's number in my phone book, and I didn't think he would still have the same number so I rang him. He answered and I asked him if he still remembered me? I'm happy to say, he did. I gave him my condolences for his sad loss and then hung up. Then the voice started again. I said 'give me a break, I have done what you asked'. This time I sent him a text asking if he would like to come to dinner, which he accepted. We got on really well that evening and I asked him why he had been so rude all those years ago. He replied that he had fallen in love with me back in 1994 and didn't trust himself to be 'just good friends' with me. He was being faithful and true to his wife which I commend him for. I know that some people said that we were having an affair when his wife was still alive and terminally ill. We never did though.

There was one thing I had to go through concerning my landlords. The six-month tenancy was coming up for renewal and the landlord asked me if we could sign a contract with another company but I had to lie and empty my flat of all of my belongings. In other words, move out and back in again. I was placed in a very difficult position and had to comply, although thinking about it now I shouldn't have. It was so stressful and on top of that I had to get another deposit together whilst I was waiting for the other one to come back. Never ever again will I ever help out a landlord. They only seem to do things for their own gain.

It was February 2009 when Richard proposed to me and I immediately said yes. I'd already said I would never marry again but I knew he was the right person for me. I don't know how my family felt about my marrying again but I do know that Melissa's family turned on Richard and accused him of having an affair whilst their mother was ill and they became rather nasty. This really upset him as he had only ever tried to do the right thing by them. The only thing about someone coming into your life when you lose someone is that there is no right or wrong timing. It doesn't mean that you have stopped loving your loved one, it just means that you feel things in a different way. I know I helped Richard through his grief and I was meant to be there to help him. No one see's how that person is coping when they are alone and just because Richard was not crying all the time in public he was accused of being heartless. Grief is a painful private thing, we all deal with it the best way we can.

We were married in September 2010. The morning was bright sunshine, Murrey came and collected me and we had a lovely journey to the register office as I felt it was a mother and son moment. I was so nervous! Murrey walked me down the aisle and

Richard didn't turn round once, he didn't say much either, I wasn't sure of what he was thinking or feeling.

The day was absolutely wonderful. We were blessed with the love of our family and friends and I can honestly say it was one of the happiest day of my life. We were married at Rochester Register Office and had our blessing on the same day at a Spiritualist Church in Gillingham. It was our family and friends that made the day for us and we received wonderful wedding gifts. I must mention here about Maria and Mel. They were a godsend with regards to getting the wedding reception sorted, Maria did the cooking and Mel helped with the running around and ideas too. It couldn't have gone better, they were brilliant.

It was amazing how I met Mel. This is another example of spirit bringing people into your life. Maria had a friend called Lorna living on the Isle of Sheppey and Maria thought it would be a good idea for us to meet for lunch. We'd arranged where we were meeting and Lorna asked if it would be okay to bring along a friend of hers as she was interested in Spiritualism. Maria and I were introduced to Mel and we hit it off straight away and had a lovely afternoon. Mel gave me a lift home and we talked about meeting up again. Mel was going through a difficult time of her own and she felt comfortable in coming round to my flat and it was then she met Nigel too. Both Nigel and I helped Mel in some way and also to help her develop her spiritual gifts and understand that what she was feeling was normal. We introduced her to healing and she has the ability. The trouble with Mel is that she doesn't believe in herself and I'm afraid there are so many out there who are going through the very same thing. The trouble with spiritual healing nowadays is that you need certificates for this insurance or for that. The whole process appears to have become a money making venture for those who seek to regulate the Healing Ministry under the guise of following the law. I get so frustrated when I hear about wonderful healers who have stopped practicing because they don't have the right papers or certificates and/or they can't afford to pay for a healing course. Healers are not all the same. You can't train someone to be a healer.

You can only suggest examples of best practice as everybody heals in different ways. I nearly stopped training for my healing certificate when I started reading about all the regulations and the do's and don'ts. The bureaucracy beggar's belief, and this has all come about because society has become so litigious that healers feel they have to cover themselves in case some ill-intentioned person with their eye on the main chance tries to sue them. Sad to say, Spiritualism and spiritual healing are not what they used to be. In some respects, the movement has lost its way and become too preoccupied with legal niceties and with money. I feel that too many followers of the spiritual pathway have lost sight of the true meaning of their faith.

Mel's friend Lorna was also going through a hard time. Her second marriage had broken down and she was having difficulties coping. Obviously this was causing great concern to both Maria and Mel and we all tried to help her. It was in the spring of 2009 when Maria rang me. She was distraught and said 'she's done it'. Not being entirely sure what Maria meant I calmed her down and she told me that Lorna had hung herself. It was Lorna's parents who found her, you can't imagine how they must have felt seeing their daughter like that. She'd made an excuse to go back to her flat to collect some things and no one was able to contact her after she had failed to turn up when she said she would. They eventually broke into the flat and found her hanging in the bathroom. Poor Lorna. She was in deep depression; no one could reach her to bring her back. It hurt so many of her friends and loved ones as I know we felt that we had failed her in some way.

I would like to touch upon the subject of suicides. Of late, when I've been giving demonstrations of mediumship, a number of people who have taken their own lives have come through, wishing to communicate. These souls invariably wish to say sorry for what they have done and apologise for any pain they have caused. Some recipients of such messages gain a sense of release or closure while others experience anger. Suicide can be a very difficult issue to deal with and there are many differing opinions on how it should be approached. I've read many books about the spirit world and reincarnation and what follows is my personal understanding of the subject. Some people strongly believe that suicide is for cowards. However even if you feel that you know how such a person must have felt, this seems to me to be a harsh judgement. For myself, I know what it's like to be in such a lonely and painful place that suicide seems to be the only possible solution. All you can see and feel is your own despair. When you can't see a way forward or an alternative way out, the last thing you need is somebody saying 'come on, snap out of it, it's not that bad' or 'there are people worse off than you'. I'm sure such people mean well, but they are not living in your own private hell and rarely have any idea of your true feelings.

I believe that those who have taken their own lives go to a place of healing where they are given the chance to review their actions on the Earth plane. They gain an understanding of what could have happened if they'd stayed and worked through their pain, of the knock-on effects of their actions on their family and friends and on others. If a person decides to end their own life early because they can't cope with a task they've chosen to undertake or other adverse circumstances, their spirit guides won't be happy at the wasted development opportunity. A person committing suicide is not judged by God or some other higher power but is given the chance to judge themselves. There is also another side to all this which some may find difficult to comprehend. A person deciding to end their life is by no means unique as many others have suffered from similar feelings including myself. Such a person could decide on this course of action because it's written in their blue print, part of their karmic journey, or because it's simply another lesson that has to be learnt to help their own soul group develop. They may have chosen this pathway out of love for a soul group member they are trying to help on the earth plane. I'm sure this won't make sense to some, but it made sense to me during my studies about the Spirit world and soul groups. For those interested in further reading around this subject, there are some fantastic books on the subject of the spirit world and reincarnation, such as *Realms of the Earth Angels* by Doreen Virtue,

Destiny of Souls by Michael Newton and *The Realm of Spirits* by Hugo van den Dool.

Steven had already got married two months before my marriage to Richard and was spending six months in a Thai elephant sanctuary as part of his honeymoon. Our relationship had been distant since I left his father Martin and I felt he had never forgiven me for that break up. I don't blame Steven in any way for having these thoughts and emotions. These events took place at the most difficult time of his life when he was going into puberty and I allowed Charles to influence our relationship. I should have put my three children first and I have no real excuses for my failure to do so. Steven did ring me while I was having my make-up done on the morning of my wedding to Charles which made me cry as I'm sure you can imagine.

Murrey had got engaged to a wonderful girl who went on to qualify as a nurse. They are a fantastic couple and we all look forward to their wedding in October 2016.

Now back to my wedding to Richard. We didn't have a honeymoon straight away, we went away in the following April. What we did do was move Richard out of his house and into my flat. We didn't live together until we were married, old fashioned I know but it really did work for us. I really enjoyed being married again, it wasn't all plain sailing, there are bound to be teething problems and it's all the fun of finding out about and getting used to each other.

The wonderful thing about Richard is that he is a working medium too. We are so compatible in so many ways and we have an understanding of each other's spiritual journey. We are able to help each other when we become down or disillusioned with regards to our spiritual work, we are there for each other to work through it. I feel we are lucky as it makes our lives comfortable. I'm aware of people who are in the spiritual movement whose partners are not in the spiritual way of life and this can make it rather difficult for them or put a strain on their relationship.

I used to run two circles in the flat and we all really enjoyed them and made some wonderful friends. Once Richard and I were married, our bookings from churches for rostrum work increased. We really did struggle with this at times as we didn't have a car. We had to travel by bus and/or train. What many people didn't realise was how long it would take us to get to some of the churches/centres we served. There were times when we left home at three in the afternoon and didn't get back home till ten thirty at night. When you think about it that's nearly an eight hour day. I will talk more about churches etc. in another chapter.

Richard and I were very happy living in the flat until the landlords began making our lives very uncomfortable in 2013 by having an extension built upstairs. We had holes in the wall, water pouring through the ceiling and many other things and they were not prepared to reduce our rent or to help us in any way. Our privacy was being trampled on, we'd have builders walking through our rooms, looking through windows and I was reduced to living in one room and couldn't use the kitchen. We also had to clean everything when they left each evening. We were even accused by the builders of doing or saying things about them to the landlords which caused them to walk off the job. I think it was an excuse because the landlords were making their lives difficult. It was all one way, theirs. It was so bad that I couldn't take it anymore and persuaded Richard to let us move. I started looking for a place and Nigel was helping me by driving me to the places. Richard told me just to go and find a place and whatever I found, it would be okay with him. In fact, Richard never saw the house until the day we moved in and I'm happy to say that he loved it. It was perfect for him to walk to the station to catch the London-bound train for his work. The house proved to be perfect in many ways.

Just before we moved. I was running a circle and one of my students mentioned that a lady was going to be closing her spiritual centre in Rainham. Whilst my students were in their meditation, an idea was forming in my head, why I don't know as I had no intention of running a centre. After the circle had closed and I was on my own, I rang the lady and asked her what was happening as I was due to serve there in a couple of weeks. She explained and before you knew it this mouth of mine said 'how would you feel if I took it over'. I swear I have someone controlling my voice box. I cleared it with Richard and he gave me his blessing and two weeks after we moved into our new home, I opened my very own Spiritualist Centre in the Old Oast House adjacent to Rainham station.

CHAPTER 9

The opening night of the centre was a great success. All of my friends were there to help and support me. I absolutely loved running the centre and meeting different people. Running your own centre is very hard work, you have to keep advertising, booking mediums and taking care of them, run the kitchen, think up new ideas for the centre etc. Some ideas failed but many were successful. We also held some great fundraising events for different charities, I especially loved the Christmas celebration at the centre as we usually had a bring and share supper along with the singing of carols. Brilliant. I was hiring a hall in an old oast house which had been turned into a community centre. This is a fantastic place to be as there are parking spaces and plenty of rooms to go into if you wish to expand the centre.

The one thing about the place is that it's very active with spirit entities. There were a couple of nasty one's there and we dealt with them by moving them on. We also asked those who were still stuck on the Earth plane if they wished to go to the light and this we did. We asked for protection for ourselves, prayed for the Angels to come forward and show the light bringing a loved one who has gone before them to help them realise that they don't have to stay where they are on the Earth plane. They do tend to go once they realise they are free to do so. There are some who just cannot see this and choose to stay which is sad. They become so attached to the Earth and are unable to see the pure beauty of what is on the 'other side'. You may be saying "what is there on the other side?" From the books I've read and from what my guides have told me; what is on the other side is unimaginable beauty, release from pain and torment, pure love, meeting of our loved ones who have gone before us. There is beautiful music, joy, the feeling of being you, the feeling of a job well done to help your soul's growth. We are free to do anything or go anywhere with no restrictions of our earthly body. The subject is endless and magical at the same time.

Richard and I eventually managed to buy a car after saving up very hard for it which made our lives so much easier. Willow had also settled down well too. Richard and I would go to see his parents who lived in Wales. Richard's mother was Welsh and his father was from London. They had retired to west Wales many years before. They were wonderful people and I loved them dearly and they made me feel so welcomed. We had some really good times there. Life was wonderful until 2014 then Spirit really did put Richard and me to the test.

Richard's mother was having problems with her leg after she'd had a fall. The hospital couldn't find anything wrong with it but it was getting progressively worse. Eventually they noticed she had gangrene on a couple of her toes and suggested she go into hospital to have them removed. In the end she was moved from one hospital which was only thirteen miles from her home to another which was eighty miles away in Swansea. The hospital told Richard that his mother was going to have her leg amputated above the knee. As you can imagine it was a shock to all the family and very stressful for his father. Richard's father travelled to Swansea every single day to be with her. I went with Richard one time to see her and was quite shocked at how she had aged and withered away.

During this time I was having some problems of my own. I had a couple of episodes when my vision would become blurred and would lose the colour. I would become very forgetful, just couldn't remember what I was going to say or what I was thinking off. I just used to laugh it off and put it down to getting old. I happen to mention it to Amy and Maria and they very forcefully told me to make an appointment with the doctor. Usually I just go 'yeah, yeah, one day' but this time something told me to get on with it.

My doctor was absolutely brilliant and I owe a lot to her. After I'd described what my symptoms were she said, "Just to be on the safe side we'll book you in for a CT scan." Having the scan was weird. I wasn't aware that I was to have this dye injected into my arm and was warned that I might feel as if I was wetting myself and that I would go hot and maybe the heart rate might go up a little bit. I did indeed feel the 'wetting' and I did feel slightly panicky when the old heart rate went up but I thought about the Angels and calmed down. I was told to ring the doctors back to get my results. I just thought it would all be normal and that they would find nothing.

It was August and Richard's mum deteriorated to such an extent that she was moved to a hospital closer to home. Richard knew if she was moved there she wouldn't be coming out again, and so it proved. Mum passed away peacefully on 20th August 2014. She just didn't want to live with having half her leg taken away and simply gave up.

I'd already had the appointment booked with the doctor the next day (21st August) as I was asked to come in to see her with regards to my CT scan results. I was so thankful I had Richard with me. The doctor told me I had a Meningioma at the back of my brain – a brain tumour on the lining of the brain at the back of my head on the left-hand side. How can I explain what my feelings were when I was given the news? The doctor did say that this kind of tumour is normally benign and I would recover from it. She was brilliant when it came to making the appointment to see the specialist; the available appointments were so far away that she pulled some strings and I went to see the specialist in September.

When I came out of the doctors and was walking towards the exit of the building it suddenly hit me. I turned to Richard and said 'why me'. We were both in shock and I was worried about Richard because he was having to go through it all again. His late wife Melissa passed with a brain tumour and he thought he was going to lose me in the same way. When I got home I just howled, my soul was hurting, I was hurting. I was so angry; 'why me' kept coming into my mind. I did go through all the emotions, thinking about what if I died, how my family was going to cope. My children were the first people I told of my illness. I don't know how they felt, but they were very strong and positive for me. I know Richard was not coping very well but was putting on such a brave face.

I went through some very dark nights. Night times are the worst as your mind goes on overdrive. The 'what if's kick in and you start to think how can I beat this, there must be another way around of not going through this and in the end there isn't a way round. You have to deal with it and deal with it face on.

I nearly parted with spirit because of what I had to go through. I thought I'd suffered enough. It felt as if I was being tested yet again.

Before seeing the specialist we went to Richard's mother's funeral. It was a very sad day but a beautiful one if you can understand my meaning. The weather was lovely until we were on our way to the wake. The scenery surrounding the crematorium was beautiful, the chapel had a huge glass window overlooking a Welsh valley; very fitting for Richard's mum.

I went to see the specialist at Darenth Valley Hospital near Dartford in Kent who did some tests to see what effect the tumour was having on me and she decided to make an appointment for me to have an MRI scan. This was done in a private clinic attached to St. Mary Hospital, Sidcup. On arrival I was given a form and a folder to choose what music I would like to listen to whilst in the MRI machine. You need the music, as I could hear the noise of the machine humming away and it sounded like the machine was going through a wash cycle on fast spin! I had this done in October. One thing I can say about the treatment I got once my condition was diagnosed, they were very quick in giving me my appointments. My next appointment for the results of the MRI was to see a consultant at Kings College Hospital in London. I saw a Professor at Kings and he was really lovely. He explained everything to me and because of the size of the tumour suggested that it would be best for me to undergo an operation to have it removed. It was quite a big one at nearly four cm across. They planned to perform the operation in January 2015. There was a time when I so nearly changed my mind in having the operation. The risks was overwhelming, like, having a severe stroke, heart attack, losing my sight completely, and losing my hearing, or worst still I could die on the operating table. But then I had to think, what did I have to lose? As the Professor said, I was young enough now to get through it a lot easier than if I'd waited another five or ten years.

People are amazing. We had the most fantastic support from everyone we knew. I asked for healing prayers and the response was overwhelming. I was also taking a course with the Corinthian Healing Association to gain my healing certificate and I received a lot of healing there too. I truly believe it was the healing I was receiving that got me through it all.

I'd also made a decision to hand over the centre to somebody else as I just didn't know what the outcome of my operation would be. It was a heart breaking decision as I felt it was something that I'd succeeded at. Again I was angry at spirit. It seems everything I start has to stop or it gets taken away from me. I was told months later the reason for this which I will explain further on in the book. It all made sense and it was a real light bulb moment, I can tell you.

After my initial anger, I became calmer and more positive. I changed my thoughts and I believe it went a long way to helping me. I know there are some who would say 'it's easy for you to say' but I know me, I'm a fighter. I always go down for a short while and then say "enough is enough, this will not get me anywhere" and start thinking and doing positive things.

We finally got the operation date, it was on 21st January 2015, my daughter's birthday. Amy had always said it would be on that date and she was right. I did suggest that I should put off the operation until a later date, but Amy said no. On the appointed day, Richard and I were to wait for the phone call telling us to come into hospital. When the call came, Richard and I turned to each other and had a little cry and said 'this is it'. What my family were going through must have been hard for them.

It was in December of 2013 that the children nearly lost their father Martin. He had a massive heart attack, so serious that the consultant was amazed that he lived through it. Again we sent him a lot of healing prayers. Steven even came home from Australia where he was looking for work and planned to stay there for a year. Unfortunately, his marriage didn't last so he went on to make a fantastic new life for himself and has done some amazing and scary things. I envy him. Now the children had to go through the trauma of seeing their mother go through this major operation.

Richard and I arrived at the hospital ward, I was shown into a room which was mine for the night. We were making small talk, both of us alone with our own thoughts. I was still feeling calm. I had a lot of prodding and poking and was asked a lot of questions. Surgeons came and went, doctors came and shaved some of my hair to attached paddings for the probes around my head. I had another CT scan and then finally I was left alone. Richard had already left for home. I knew he would be opening a bottle and not sleeping much. He didn't know if I was going to make it. Also this was bringing so many memories back as his late wife Melissa had stayed on the very same ward as I did.

I did manage to get some sleep. They woke me up at six to get me to have a shower and get ready. The nurses thought I would be going down to theatre in the morning. I waited and waited and my blood pressure was going up and up, even though I seemed calm but my heart was saying different. The orderlies came to get me at two p.m. I was wheeled down to theatre in my bed and then the three surgeons came and introduced themselves to me; two I'd already met previously but not the third. When I was outside the main theatre doors, I had this amazing calmness come over me. I just knew I was going to be okay, I was going to see my loved ones again. I was wheeled in and was talking briefly to the anaesthetist and turned to look at the wall, then I saw the light going down the wall and I was asleep.

The next thing I remember was briefly waking up in the recovery room as they were wheeling me back onto the ward. It was nine thirty p.m.

Poor Richard and Amy; they were beside themselves with worry and not having any news about how the operation was going. It was really lovely seeing them again, I was chatting away, and god knows what I was saying as I must have still been under the anaesthetic. They were laughing at my 'bee hive' bandages around my head. I was relieved to see Richard there and Amy too. The strain on his face told me everything I needed to know. They left that night to catch the last train home. Murrey had already said he would pick them up if they wanted to stay longer, but I wasn't very coherent and I was sleepy.

You wouldn't believe the worst bit about the pain. It wasn't my head; it was my neck. Apparently this resulted from the position of my head being held in for a long time whilst they cut my skull to get to the tumour. I still suffer with it at times now. I loved the taste of the morphine. It tasted like raspberry, yummy!

I wasn't much use the next day, I was very sleepy and even slept most of the time whilst Amy and Murrey were visiting me. I did feel guilty as they came all the way up to London to see me. Amy did bring me my favourite food, gypsy tart, but I couldn't face it though. In fact I couldn't eat much of the food at the hospital, it was disgusting so I stuck with the yogurt. Richard was lovely and again I ignored him most of the night, bless him.

On the Friday morning, the consultants came round and said I could go home! I phoned Richard and gave him my news and he was surprised too. I had to do a few things before I was allowed to come home. I had to walk the stairs, go to the toilet, walk a certain distance and pick up objects from the floor. If the nurses, auxiliaries and doctors had read my notes they would have known I was both deaf and partially blind! The number of times I had to keep telling them of my condition because they had not read my notes exceeded the grains of sand on Brighton beach! Mind you, they were surprised because of the way I coped with my sight and hearing problems. I was clever at hiding these disabilities.

You just wouldn't believe the orderly when it came to my leaving the ward to go home. Richard had come to fetch me and the orderly wheeled me down to the main lobby of the hospital. Richard told the orderly that he would go and get the car thinking that the orderly would stay with me. Bearing in mind I'd just had major brain surgery, the orderly just left me there. We were both angry at this lack of care. It was so nice to get home.

That first night of being at home was frightening. It was in the early hours of the morning when I needed to go to the bathroom. I managed to walk out of the bedroom and then I panicked as I just didn't know where the bathroom was, I was totally lost. I was feeling around the walls trying to find the doors and even when I did, I didn't know where it was in relation to what room it was. I called out to Richard to help me and he guided me into the bathroom. You may be asking 'why didn't she turn the light on?' The light switch was about six feet from our bedroom door and I was so used to walking around the house without lights on due to my eye condition.

Richard had to go to work but my darling friend Maria came up to stay with us to look after me and she did this lovely pamper day for me, we were spoilt with her home cooking. I will always be grateful to her. I had some wonderful cards and flowers. I also told my Aunt Sandra what I had gone through, I couldn't tell her sooner as she had lost her brother, my uncle, earlier in the year. I'd told her eldest daughter just in case anything happened to me.

I made a full recovery with the help and love of my darling husband, family and friends. I did receive good news when I went for my first check-up. The professor had said that I'd made a great recovery and that the operation had turned out better than they had hoped. When they had got to the tumour they had discovered it was attached to a main vein in the brain and if they had to remove it completely I could have suffered a severe stroke, so they had left a nodule behind and the chance of this growing back is as little as two percent. All I kept doing was hugging the professor and crying with relief. Needless to say we left the hospital and went to the nearest bar and celebrated. We were only doing what the professor said, go and live your life to the full!

But, there is another ongoing side to this. Because I'd put on such a brave face, coped with everything, put others before myself, I'm suffering emotionally to the extent I've asked for counselling for the first time in my life. For the first time I'm absolutely scared of dying. Me? Being a Spiritualist, having the communication and understanding of the spirit world, Yes, me. This has caused me to suffer with anxiety, anxiety that had been locked away in my sub-conscious mind has finally exploded and now I have to deal with this.

This has made me realise how precious life is, live it as if it's going to be your last day, and you never know what is around the corner.

Now I'm on my next adventure. Richard retired in February of 2015 and we now have a wonderful future ahead of us.

CHAPTER 10

You may be wondering how I have managed to cope with everything that has gone on. I sometimes ask the very same question. All I know is that there is more to life and purpose than I can understand. It was only recently that everything began to fall into place and now I do understand the reason why I'm here on the Earth plane.

The one thing I have discovered about myself due to things that have been brought to the surface since my operation is that I'm suffering from PTSD (Post Traumatic Stress Disorder). Many of you would be thinking that this is something associated with being involved in war situations, but this is not always so.

It all came about when I started having anxiety attacks and fearing death. I became so frightened of it that I was waking up during the early hours of the morning unable to breathe, shaking, heart racing, so much so that I had to go downstairs and do something to take my mind off it. It got bad and I spoke to a friend of mine about it and she suggested that I should do a self-referral to have counselling.

The counselling has been such an eye opener. I have been deeply affected by those occasions in my life when I have had no control over particular situations. I didn't have control over my brain tumour, I had to put my faith and trust in the doctors to help get rid of it. It also came out that what Eric had done to me in the past is still there in the back of my mind. Silly little things can trigger a negative reaction and behaviour and I don't know why this should be happening. Now I'm beginning to understand how situations in the past and my reactions to them have led me to where I am today.

All I can say about abusers, any abusers, is that they really need to think about what they are doing, the long term effect they have on other human beings. You can destroy a person just for your own self-gratification and they are the ones who have to live with their own pain and trauma for the rest of their lives. Some of us are very strong, for which I count my blessings but there are many who are not so lucky.

Looking back over my life I know I have made many mistakes; who hasn't? It takes a special person to acknowledge their mistakes and to try to rectify them. There are some things that you cannot change no matter how hard you try and that's when you just have to accept things and walk away.

My biggest regret is that I put my children through so much pain when I left their father Martin. But, when you are going through a particular situation, you cannot see beyond your own pain and how you might get out of it. However, was I helping my children to grow and become who they are today or was I learning a very big lesson from past life issues that I didn't address then?

What I have learnt, up to now, is that I was a very lonely person. So lonely that I've sat and cried so many times because of being trapped in my situation and my disability. There never seemed a way out. Families today have become so insular, so wrapped up in their own lives and trying to live in today's world. There is no time for others anymore. In the past you always had your favourite gran or granddad, aunt or uncle; people you could turn to within the family. All of that has gone. I've always regretted that I never knew my real father or either of my grandparents. I never had a role model within the family unit. I feel I had to grow up by myself and learn things the hard way. Mum didn't have a role model either as her family was torn apart. Life in those days was harsher with strict discipline so that you didn't go and talk to your parents about your fears or what was happening to you. There wasn't the television and media that you have today where you gain knowledge and an ability to bring things out into the open. In the '50s and '60s, people were starting to become aware of social behaviour, they were beginning to rebel and to have a voice to protest. We were beginning to have our freedom after so many years of restrictions dating back to the Victorian era. Mum never ever taught me the right or wrong way of life, bless her, she didn't know then either. We learn from our parents and if they don't know themselves, how can they teach us?

It was through Spiritualism that my eyes were opened to everything that had been going on around me. It was noticing how much my guides and the Angels were in my life helping me and guiding me, hearing that voice in my head when I needed it. You won't believe this, but I didn't believe in Angels or understand them. I kept buying books and things that were to do with Angels then put them away and never picked them up to read or work with. I even named my business 'Fallen Angels'. It was the Angels who were trying so hard to get my attention and I'm happy to say, they've finally succeeded. Phew! I hear them say. I was told by a medium friend of mine when I was speaking to her about my Angel connection, that my name meant Angel Messenger and that I was an Earth Angel'. It was whilst I was taking part in a Numerology workshop that everything finally fell into place. Before you come back to the Earth plane, you have agreed to undertake certain tasks and the tutor told me my task was to help and serve humanity. That was why I kept giving things up, and not completing things that I've started. I just cried with relief as it all made sense to me. It also explains why I just 'know' without understanding why.

The trouble with me was that I didn't value who I was. You ask the question when someone says to you that you are special. Your first response is 'who me? Why me?' The answer is, why not you? What is difficult, is understanding the 'agreement' with the spirit world to undertake certain challenges, and help certain people on their soul journey. You are part of a soul group that has undertaken these challenges to help each other to develop and grow.

When I look back upon my life I realise that I have helped many people on their own journey and they have helped me in their turn. There have been people there just when I needed them. To show an example. In 2015 Richard and I were involved in a head-on collision with a foreign driver who forgot what side of the road he was on. Luckily for the both of us we were approaching a blind bend and going slowly. Obviously it was such a shock when the two cars collided. When I was getting out of the car I just happened to look at the side of a removal lorry passing the scene of the incident, and there right across the side of the lorry was my best friend Nigel's surname. Now his name is unusual and we haven't come across it before until this day. I phoned him and he was an Angel as he came out and helped us and got us home. I always protect us and the car before we ever start a car journey. The Angels were there with us that day. It could have been worse but luckily we didn't sustain any injuries at all.

The amazing thing is that the Angels have always been there whenever I have had a crisis, needed help, and needed healing for myself and others. They are wonderful silent workers for humankind, if only we would trust them and acknowledge them. It's taken me' till now to do so, and to acknowledge too that I am an Earth Angel.

I'm still continuing to serve Spiritual churches/centres, but I'm becoming very disillusioned with the way the movement is going. I've come across many things which have shocked me and can't believe that they should be allowed. What Richard and I have to do before we do a service is to find out what the protocol of the church is. Some don't say prayers, some don't want you to mention the word 'God' or have anything to do with religion, but it's okay to say the Lord's Prayer. We went to one place where the lady in charge was adamant that they were not a church or spiritual centre. We were instructed in no uncertain terms not to say prayers and not to mention religion. She told us that she ran a teaching centre. Now, my belief is when working with spirit, you should be protected and should teach others to do likewise. You just don't know what you are attracting from the spirit world. There are so many lost souls and evil entities that you can attract to you. When you open yourself to spirit you are a beacon of light saying I'm here, come to me.

You just won't believe the number of requests to clear spirits from people's homes that Nigel and I have received. I know my limits. If I sense the entity is beyond my power to deal with I will not touch it. Nigel deals with them for me; we co-operate in this work.

Many people I've come across think this is all a game, (it's not); or they want to learn the basics (if they do) and say I'm a medium and go out delivering messages. There is such a fine line we are walking on, you can do tremendous harm to another person if you have not been trained. It's not a five minute wonder. I've heard some say they want to be famous and get all the money that the famous mediums are getting. Let them do so. What you have to understand, as much as spirit give you the 'gifts' they can also take them away if you abuse them. It may not happen straight away but it will. I've seen this happen and the person/s involved were never able to work again.

Being a Medium carries great responsibility. When you are running a circle teaching your students, you have to make them understand that they need to learn the boring bits first. It's those boring bits that may save them a lot of heartache in the long run. I'll give you an example. I had a mature man who came to my circle and he had joined several others. In my circle, Nigel and I used to teach about the importance of protection, opening and closing your chakra centres down etc. He used to argue with us and just couldn't understand why we should do this as the other circles didn't believe in this. Spirit taught him a lesson to try and make him understand. Nigel and I began to notice that he wasn't looking too good and we had also picked up that he had a bad entity attached to him. Eventually the mature student realised that he wasn't feeling too good and asked Nigel for help. Nigel had to remove two entities from him and his home. After he had done this, the student was a lot brighter and happier. Until the next time. Again Nigel did the clearance work as the student still hadn't learnt about protection. The final straw came when the student came to the circle and he was sitting next to me and all I wanted to do was get him out of the house. The anger I was feeling was incredible. I had to go round my home to cleanse it and cleanse myself. I stopped him from coming to the circle as he was not learning his lesson. He was listening to the other circles saying that Nigel and I didn't know what we were talking about. If only they knew!

You may be asking the question, what is a circle? When Richard first started going to a spiritualist church they kept mentioning about joining a circle. He began to wonder what it was as his idea of a circle was a secret society of some sorts. Well, a circle is when you are invited to learn how to develop your spiritual connections and to give off messages. You learn to connect with your guides, loved ones in spirit, Angels, etc. and you are mostly sitting on chairs in a circle. So, if you feel you wish to go further with your development, my advice is to find a Spiritualist church close to you and they will be able to help and guide you.

The thing that Richard and I (and other mediums that we have spoken to) are disheartened about is the lack of respect for Mediums who have taken their time to come from where ever they are living to serve a church/centre. We are not valued for our commitment to the church and people that we have undertaken to help. We have arrived at the venue and there is a lack of welcome; no offer of a drink. At the end of the service, there have been times when we don't get a drink. When I began serving, you used to have sandwiches and drink laid on for you. You need this to help in the grounding of yourself once you have been working with spirit. It may have been a long time since you have eaten and it will be late when you return home, by this time you can be quite tired. Richard used to serve churches after he had done a day's work, he hadn't had time to eat and all he would get was a biscuit and arrive home just before eleven at night having been up since five a.m.

Why have churches/centres become so, so money orientated? It's the Mediums that keep their doors open. Without them, they won't have a church. Mediums, healers and teachers are the backbone of the spiritual movement who are dedicated in the work we have chosen to undertake, it's not the famous mediums, it's the unknown silent workers. It's supposed to be about serving God, Spirit and humanity. There have been times when we've just been handed an envelope containing money that barely cover our expenses; and a lot of mediums have noticed that fees are going down. Having said all of this, we have been receiving many calls asking us to step in for one reason or other. Mediums are cancelling their booking left, right and centre, maybe they too have become disheartened as I know Richard and I have been so close to walking away from it all.

What is also so sad is seeing and hearing about the internal bickering that goes on. He said this, she said that. It's sounding like children in a school playground. There is supposed to be unity and love within the Spiritualist movement; now it's all to do with the ego. There have been times when I think our movement is no better than any other religious movement. I thought we were supposed to be above all of that. I thought we were meant to be here to help and support one another not to put up with the divisions that now plague our movement. I do wonder at times where it's all going to end up. Maybe we should take time to think about this and address the problems before it's too late. We were sent here to change the negativity of the world to love and peace not fuel that same negativity.

There are a lot of people out there who are looking for help, answers, especially to those who wish to develop their spiritual and healing gifts, and they just don't know where to turn to. Maybe we should become more aware of these people and be ready to guide them. Let us not forget the youngsters. They are being pushed aside. I've come across many youngsters who have been going through something terrible with regards to 'seeing', hearing things and they are thinking they are going mad. It's such a relief to them when they discover what the real reasons are. We need to be there for them, after all, they are our future.

Both Nigel and I have had to help those who have been dabbling with the Ouija board thinking that it's a good laugh. No it's not. You do have to learn to protect yourself and to have someone who is a qualified Medium to be able to work with the board. You just do not know who you are inviting in. We had a case once when we had a young lady come to us and she said her life had gone terribly wrong since she worked the board. Her relationship failed, her partner took the children away, she kept losing her jobs, her home and she had severe depression to the point that she contemplated ending her life.

We discovered she had a very nasty 'entity' attached to her and moved it off her. She is now a lot better and has a greater understanding as to why she was suffering. As in anything, do not touch anything that you don't have any understanding, knowledge or training in. It will save so much heartache.

Well, I've come to the end of this book. I've learnt a lot, seen a lot, met a lot of people, done a lot and I dare say there is still a lot more to be done. I wanted to show you that you can survive, you can ask God for help. It may not be what you want but it will be what you need for your soul's journey.